The Artistry of Preaching Series

Actuality

Real Life Stories for Sermons That Matter

For My Colleague Ruth Boen!

12-2-14

Scott Hoezee

T0204237

Abingdon Press
Nashville

ACTUALITY:
REAL LIFE STORIES FOR SERMONS THAT MATTER

Copyright © 2014 by Abingdon Press

This book is printed on acid-free paper.

Library of Congress Cataloging-in-Publication Data

Hoezee, Scott, 1964–
    Actuality : real life stories for sermons that matter / by Scott Hoezee.
        pages cm. — (The artistry of preaching ; 2)
    ISBN 978-1-4267-6593-3 (paperback : alk. paper) 1. Preaching. 2. Experience. 3. Sermons. I. Title.
    BV4211.3.H637 2014
    251—dc23

                                                                        2014022857

Scripture quotations unless otherwise noted are taken from the Holy Bible, New International Version®, NIV®. Copyright © 1973, 1978, 1984, 2011 by Biblica, Inc.™ Used by permission of Zondervan. All rights reserved worldwide. www.zondervan.com. The "NIV" and "New International Version" are trademarks registered in the United States Patent and Trademark Office by Biblica, Inc.™

14 15 16 17 18 19 20 21 22 23—10 9 8 7 6 5 4 3 2 1

MANUFACTURED IN THE UNITED STATES OF AMERICA

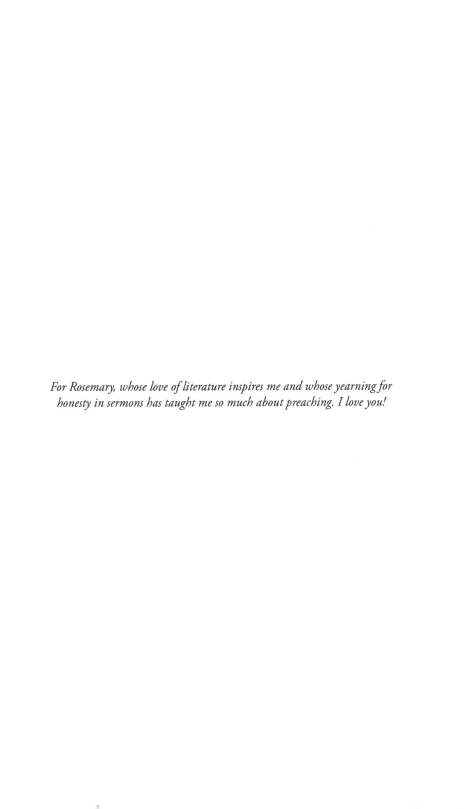

For Rosemary, whose love of literature inspires me and whose yearning for honesty in sermons has taught me so much about preaching. I love you!

Contents

Contents

Series Preface

The Artistry of Preaching series gives practical guidance on matters that receive insufficient attention in preaching literature yet that are key for preachers seeking greater creativity in their preaching. Fresh, faithful proclamation requires imagination and creative engagement of the Bible and our world. There is no shortage of commentaries on the Bible and books on biblical interpretation for preaching, but practical resources to help strengthen the creativity of preachers to help them better to proclaim the gospel are much in need.

The first volume of this series, *Preaching as Poetry: Beauty, Goodness, and Truth in Every Sermon*, redefines preaching for our current postmodern age. Imagination is needed to compose strong theological sermons. Modernist notions of authority, goodness, and truth are challenged by our current culture. The church needs to adapt to a new world, where faith is understood as poetry rooted in the beauty, goodness, and truth of a saving relationship with God.

The second and current volume of the series, *Actuality: Real Life Stories for Sermons That Matter*, is a resource for preachers who want guidance to be better storytellers or to use story more effectively to communicate with a new generation. Here readers will also find a collection of stories that both preach and that can stimulate their own imaginations to identify stories from their own contexts. Preachers can easily run out of good stories to use that embody the gospel. The problem is not a shortage of stories—they are all around in everyday events; the task is learning how to harvest them, as will be shown here.

Preachers long for good stories, and today's listeners are not content with the canned Internet illustrations that sound artificial and have a predictable moral. Rather, they want stories rooted in the actual world in which they live, that depict life as they know it, and that can function as Jesus's stories did, as parables and metaphors that bear God's grace to their hearers.

Scott Hoezee is a wonderful storyteller and preacher, whose insights into what makes for a good story will inspire and encourage preachers. His volume demonstrates various ways in which stories may be mined from news, literature, drama, movies, art, and daily life. He develops several key practical principles that guide his approach to biblical preaching.

The aim of the series is to be practical, to provide concrete guidelines and exercises for preachers to follow, to assist them in engaging practice. Preaching is much more than art, yet by ensuring that we as preachers employ artistry in our preaching, we assist the Holy Spirit in communicating the gospel to a new generation of people seeking God.

—Paul Scott Wilson, Series Editor

Author Preface

Years ago when I was serving as pastor of a congregation, one of our high school students met with the elders of the church to make his profession of faith. When asked what inspired him to take that important step in his faith journey, the student indicated that the main thing that got him thinking about spirituality and his own faith was a religion class assignment to write a sermon. The student then looked directly at me and said, "Turns out, it's hard to write a sermon! For a long time I thought all you did on Sunday mornings was just get up and talk!"

If only it were that easy!

Preaching is hard work. And as my colleague John Rottman has often noted when we are in the midst of grading student sermons, sermons can go wrong in a startling number of ways. Sometimes how a sermon goes wrong is very interesting, very instructive. At other times it can be hard to say why a given sermon doesn't "work," even though everyone who heard it knew that something just didn't go right.

Preaching is hard work. It has always been hard work, but the pressures of the modern world have only exacerbated the degree of difficulty. Whether it's postmodernism's sometimes squishy ideas about goodness and truth, religious pluralism that blunts ultimate claims, or the pervasive reach of the entertainment industry and its elevating of listener expectations, our present age has made the preaching craft even more fraught, more fragile than it has ever been. The average preacher also faces the unhappy truth that any number of the people who come to hear him or her on a Sunday morning might very well have spent some time in the previous week downloading YouTube videos of well-known preachers, to whom comparisons with their own pastor will inevitably be drawn.

Having preached something approaching a thousand sermons myself, I know about the pressures preachers face every week. I know, too, that without fresh infusions of good resources, images, stories, and ideas no one can preach very well for very long. A couple of years ago, a senior seminarian who was about to graduate proudly told me that the sermon he had just written for preaching class was already the eighteenth sermon he had ever written. I smiled at him as I told him that if he soon became the pastor of a congregation with both a morning and an evening service (and he soon did just that), then he'd double that sermon total in about four months' time! Buckle up! Sundays are relentless.

This is a book for all my fellow preachers. It is written in the sincere hope that it will help preachers face the challenges of our present age by writing sermons that will do exactly what most listeners in the church today desperately desire: to hear sermons that are as firmly rooted in the realities of daily life as they are deeply rooted in God's word. The series in which this book is included is called The Artistry of Preaching, and that title gets it just right: writing sermons is as much an art as a skill, as much a knack as it is a set of hard-and-fast principles.

Finding just the right story or image to fit a given Bible text in a sermon is likewise an art, a sensibility. But knowing deep down that every sermon needs just such reality-based stories is very much a principle of good preaching. Investigating how and why that is so is a big part of this volume's rationale. In the pages ahead I hope not only to make the case for a sense of "actuality" in preaching through vivid vignettes and stories, but to show what this looks like in action in ways I hope will be inspiring on a very practical, week-in and week-out level for all those preachers who know that as soon as any given sermon gets delivered, the clock is already ticking to get going on the next one!

Acknowledgments

Authors always say—because they know it's always true—that writing a book is a collaborative process. What the author comes up with across many lonely hours when it's just the writer and the computer never stays in that kind of isolation for long. Sections of the book get emailed to someone for feedback, chapters get printed up and handed off, and ultimately the whole "baggy monster" of the first draft gets tossed to some colleagues for a thorough vetting. In the case of this book, I wish to thank especially John Rottman, Kevin Adams, Mike Graves, and Paul Scott Wilson for commenting on bits and pieces of the work in progress and then finally for reading the whole manuscript. Each of these colleagues provided excellent suggestions, ideas for restructuring, and encouraging feedback that this whole project might actually be worth something. My hearty thanks to them all.

But I wish to express a kind of metathanks to a few people, too. First, I thank my longtime teacher, mentor, and friend Neal Plantinga. Anyone who is familiar with the "Imaginative Reading for Creative Preaching" seminar that Neal has led (and that I have often helped to colead) across the last dozen years—and anyone who has read Neal's own book *Reading for Preaching* (Eerdmans, 2013)—will readily recognize that a good deal of this book grew out of what I learned from Neal about how a robust program of general reading feeds the preaching life. Even twenty or so years before Neal held the first such seminar, Neal inspired me as a student to read really big and really important books like biographies by William Manchester and insightful novels by Russell Banks and Philip Roth. What's more, for the last decade I have had the privilege of directing the Center for Excellence in Preaching at Calvin Theological Seminary, and the existence of that Center is a direct result of Neal's dream and vision as seminary president to establish something that would be of real help to preachers. So heartfelt thanks to Neal for all he has taught me and all that he has brought to me.

I wish to acknowledge and thank also Paul Scott Wilson, whose acquaintance I have been privileged to make these last eight or nine years. Paul invited me to join the writers working on this Artistry of Preaching series and has given me rich opportunities to think about preaching and to learn more about the preaching craft. Paul's own books have reshaped my view of homiletics and enabled me to become a better teacher of preaching than I would have otherwise been. For all that Paul has taught me and brought to me, I thank him.

But particular thanks flow to my faculty colleague John Rottman. Although we met in passing in our seminary days and worked together from a distance on the *Word & Witness* preaching journal, we never really got to know each other until I joined the faculty at Calvin Seminary in 2005. Since then not only have we become good friends, but also John has taught me so much about preaching and preaching theory that it almost amounts to a kind of graduate school education! Across a thousand conversations about student sermons, homiletics, and our own sermons, John has helped me to expand my horizons about what it means to teach preaching, even as he has helped me to name and refine things I already knew as a result of preaching in the church for fifteen years before I came to Calvin Seminary. John is an accomplished preacher himself with twenty years of pastoral experience. He has brought so much to Calvin Seminary and also to me, and for that I thank him very sincerely and very deeply.

Thanks also to my Abingdon editor, Constance Stella, and to the whole team at Abingdon that makes it possible for books to see the light of day. Thanks to my students at Calvin Seminary these last years from whom and with whom I have learned a lot, even as I tried to help them to refine their own preaching skills. Thanks to Calvin Seminary's current president, Jul Medenblik, for his leadership and guidance and for his encouragement of me as I wrote this book. And I'd like to mention also my father-in-law, the Rev. Isaac Apol. Dad Apol passed away while I was working on this book. In his own way, he taught me a lot about preaching, too, and well into his eighties he remained an insightful commentator on the preaching craft. I miss our conversations about preaching and thank him for all he brought to my life in the quarter century I knew him.

Finally, to my wife Rosemary (to whom this book is dedicated) and to my children, Julianna and Graham, I give thanks for being the bright center of my life and for all their love and encouragement. All of that means more than any amount of words could ever hope to convey.

Introduction

There is a moment in C. S. Lewis's classic story *The Lion, the Witch, and the Wardrobe* in which the children Lucy, Edmund, Susan, and Peter—having just learned of the terrible fate that had befallen the dear faun, Mr. Tumnus, at the hands of the dreaded White Witch—are told by Mr. Beaver, "They say Aslan is on the move—perhaps has already landed."[1] And at the very mention of a name none of the children had ever heard before, their hearts were stirred. Hope seemed to have been created in them. *Aslan is on the move.* That sounded like very good news.

But then imagine that Lewis had left it at that. Imagine what a different book would have been produced if the only thing that happened after Mr. Beaver's initial announcement was having some character or another repeat—once every thirty pages or so—the line "They say Aslan is on the move," yet without ever once showing us who Aslan is and what kind of "moves" he was making. Imagine never reading about Aslan's powerful roar, or the way he later breathes on creatures like Mr. Tumnus to melt them out of the frozen stasis into which the White Witch had cursed them. Had Lewis stuck to mere description—to just *telling* readers a fact or idea or two about the great lion—Aslan would have remained a concept, an idea (and an only vaguely exciting one at that).

Lewis didn't do that. A good many sermons do. Many sermons never manage to get beyond telling us "Jesus is on the move" and never suggest what kinds of situations of need he is moving into or what in the whole wide world Jesus might do in those situations once

xv

he arrives. Aptly chosen stories drawn from real life and from those artists who have an eye for depicting the angularities of real life can head off such disconnects from reality. Finding and using just such stories are what this book is all about.

Of course, it is hardly breaking news that good stories work well in communication. It is something Jesus knew a lot about as well. That's why in his parables Jesus always simultaneously addressed people inside realistic contexts—scenarios and settings to which his every listener could relate—but then changed that situation from the inside out by revealing a larger grace at work, a grace whose goodness and power people could scarcely imagine before hearing the parable but whose possibilities seemed gloriously real *after* hearing Jesus speak. Jesus had an eye and an ear for the stories that would matter to his people to reveal both trouble and grace, need and divine action. Of all the untold ways by which we are called to apprentice ourselves to Jesus as his disciples, picking up Jesus's knack for finding stories that matter is a key portion of every preacher's apprenticeship to the Master.

I once heard Fred Craddock say that what preaching today needs is not more beauty but more reality. Craddock is not denying the proper place of stating matters clearly by way of well-chosen words, and even now and then through the elegant turn of phrase. As Paul Scott Wilson has written in this Artistry of Preaching series, having an appreciation for the power of poetry and for the ability to describe the Gospel in language that is as beautiful as the holy grace it describes is necessary and uplifting in preaching. Craddock's point seems to be more along the lines of using such language to describe not ideas and concepts shorn from real life but precisely to connect to the reality that exists outside the Sunday morning sermon. What sermons need is more reality, more actuality, more traction with the lives of the people who are doing the listening. Without this real-world connection, even beautifully eloquent speech can become just so much flowery talk. Many of us who have preached have heard the anecdote about the person who is listening to a sermon but who then observes at some point during the sermon that it had started to snow outside. This leads the listener to the observation that though the snowflakes fluttering outside the window seemed real, the sermon fluttering inside the sanctuary seemed decidedly ethereal.

That's not an observation preachers cherish!

Yet again and again as I read student sermons—but also quite often when I go back and read some of my own sermons from past years—I spy this very phenomenon. How relatively easy it is to recite great truths on a Sunday morning, but how very difficult it is to help people see what such truths would look like and feel like in their lives on the average Tuesday morning or Friday afternoon. Words like "God conquers the idols of our lives" flow quickly off the preacher's tongue. But naming even one such specific idol—and then helping the congregation know what form God's conquest of it might take—does not pass the preacher's lips as readily.

Sermons need not more flowery talk, not more words, not more slogans or aphorisms or bromides or statements; they need more reality. The congregation needs to see itself in the picture the sermon is sketching, and not just on Sunday morning while sitting in a pew, but on Wednesday morning when sitting in a corporate board meeting and on Thursday afternoon when facing a tough decision at school. The core assertion of this book centers on the contention that if sermons do not connect with the real world that real people occupy during all those hundreds of hours each week when they are not sitting in a church somewhere, then sooner or later for many people Christian faith may run the risk of seeming like a Sunday-only conceptual affair, less real than what they experience on a daily basis. Worse, the living presence of God as an active and personal presence in our lives may begin to seem merely conceptual, and that would be a singularly tragic outcome of preaching the good news!

But not everyone agrees with the assertion that stories are necessary in preaching. I have encountered students who think the biblical text needs no extra help, even as a preaching colleague once told me he thinks stories are unnecessary (he happily went on to tell me that in twenty years of preaching, he had told probably not more than five stories total). Like Karl Barth—who in theory (if not in actual practice) rejected sermonic illustrations—some today think the biblical text is both self-authenticating and self-applying. Preachers who try to help the congregation see itself in the biblical picture are just getting in the Bible's way. As quoted in William Willimon's recent book *Conversations with Barth on Preaching*, Barth asserted that not only are introductions, conclusions, and illustrations in general unnecessary, these things just generally cause "extensive" theological damage. "For what do they really involve at root? Nothing other than a search for a point of contact, for an analogue in us that can be a point of entry for the Word. . . . This is plain heresy."[2] According to Barth, the *preacher* can never create a point of contact, because only the word by the Spirit can do that. Stories and analogies in a sermon are just the preacher's attempt to be wiser than the Spirit.

But on this I most heartily disagree. Or at least I disagree that Barth is sketching a valid either-or. Of course it is ever and only the word and the Spirit that wing any sermon into people's hearts. The preacher is at best the midwife in this whole procedure. But the Spirit uses the preacher's insight and pastoral experience to do this, because otherwise one could settle for no more than the public reading of scripture and be done with it. The Bible is God's living word, but its encounter with our living world is nuanced, rich, and varied and is not the same in all times or places. Preachers absolutely must reveal the places of traction between text and world in ways that highlight the needed sense of "reality" to which Craddock points and which this book is arguing for through the use of well-chosen stories. Because what reality-based stories accomplish is not just connecting with the real lives of those listening to sermons. No, what this sense of reality does above all is bring the living presence of God into contact with life's daily experiences. And what could be a nobler goal of preaching the word of God than having the living presence of God shine through week after week?

To do otherwise runs the risk of rendering God's presence in day-to-day living remote and difficult to see. Similarly, in recent decades many of us have sadly witnessed what happens to young people who are fed a false view of scientific reality within the church (being told, for instance, how weak and thin the evidence for an old universe is). Then these students go off to college, only to discover what the real world of science looks like and how strong and thick many such claims for an old universe actually are. When the disconnect between faith and reality becomes so starkly evident to such college students, a crisis often ensues (and statistically it is a crisis in which faith becomes the losing prospect more often than not).

The claim that sermons need more reality is, therefore, far more than some preaching book slogan. The need for more reality may well be the difference between robust faith and weak faith, as one or the other is fostered through the sermons people hear on Sundays.

Stories: How and Why They Work

But how might the preacher get more of that reality into the sermon? This book is a modest attempt to answer that question, and my suggestion here is both simple and difficult: a sense of reality fills the church when sermons incorporate well-chosen stories that matter deeply to—because they resonate deeply with—the people doing the listening. Again, this is at once simple and difficult. The simple part stems from a recognition that everyone loves stories. More than abstract descriptions could ever accomplish, a well-told story typically helps people see themselves inside whatever picture the storyteller (the preacher in this case) is sketching. This is one of our most natural ways to learn, and it begins very near the beginning of all our lives.

As children, we formed our views of the world and forged our concepts of fairness not by memorizing a list of precepts our parents posted on the walls of our nurseries but through stories. We learned of the wide-ranging, never-ending nature of parental love not by hearing a lecture on that subject but by reading *The Runaway Bunny* and absorbing its lyric portrait of the reach of a mother's love for her little one. We learned about generosity not by memorizing statistics on the good that charitable giving accomplishes but by observing in a Winnie the Pooh story the selfless way that Piglet gave up his cherished home one day after the sad-sack donkey, Eeyore, moved in on the mistaken assumption that it was unoccupied space.

Stories work. They move us. They involve us. They are an integral part of everyday life. Just sit by yourself for an hour or so at Panera Bread or at Starbucks and listen in on the conversations going on all around you. Whether it's two coworkers chatting quietly about the office, a group of friends speaking animatedly about their children, or even a solo person talking on her cellphone, ninety-nine times out of a hundred what you will hear will be conversations that are almost exclusively framed by a narrative. We talk about our lives—the high points and the low points, the triumphs and the tragedies—by telling our friends and family and coworkers stories. "Well, I always knew that little Jenny was smart but listen to what happened last week in her geography class . . ." "As bosses go, I have known for some time that Mr. Philips just cannot relate to people, but then a month ago I watched how he treated his secretary and let me tell you how that unfolded . . ."

This is, therefore, the simple part of my suggestion: stories bring reality and the living presence of God into sermons because that reality is fundamentally perceived by us—and talked about by us—in narrative terms. As James K. A. Smith points out extensively in his book *Imagining the Kingdom: How Worship Works*, it has become ever more apparent to researchers that the primary way by which we apprehend and make sense of reality is not through intellection and reflective, systematic thought processes but through story. "As the novelist David Foster Wallace once put it, 'We need narrative like we need space-time; it's a built-in thing.' We are narrative animals whose very orientation to the world is fundamentally shaped by stories."[3] Story, in short, is the primary way by which we move through life and find our way through the world. This does not remove, of course, the role played by our minds. Smith, drawing off the insights of phenomenologists and social scientists, claims that it's not simply an either-or in terms of either an intellectual way to parse reality or a narrative way. We use both in a kind of "nexus" or middle space between the two—think of it as the in-between place where head and heart meet and comingle. But in that nexus location, research reveals that it is indeed story that operates as powerfully as—if not more powerfully than—sheer intellection or rational, systematic thought.

Smith points out that ultimately as Christians, what we need to be immersed in—what needs to become the overarching narrative by which we make sense of life—is the big story of God, creation, and their relation (to use Neal Plantinga's shorthand definition of "theology"). But we access that big story through a thousand little stories, each of which in its own way contributes narrative pieces to the whole. A similar point was made by numerous theologians in the latter half of the twentieth century when "narrative theology" was being developed as a new way to move theology from abstractions of doctrine toward a living, dynamic way to apprehend God. As Stephen Crites wrote in the volume *Why Narrative? Readings in Narrative Theology*, "The formal quality of experience through time is inherently narrative."[4] Crites goes on to point out that all human beings live in the "tensed modalities" of time, as our present moment is constantly moving into the future even as we live off the riches of our remembered past. "Narrative alone can contain the full temporality of experience in a unity of form."[5] Any theology that fails to understand the central place that narrative plays in the framing of human experience will finally fail at connecting with people's real lives. As Michael Root points out in that same volume, salvation itself, and the main thrust of the idea behind the phrase *Jesus saves*, can be told only in story form. "Narrative is not merely ornamental in soteriology, but constitutive."[6] Theologically and biblically, Root's assertion is robust. It is also utterly correct.

In *Imagining the Kingdom*, Smith takes similar insights and aims them squarely at not just theology proper but at the lived-out theology that is liturgy and worship. As a key component of the church's weekly worship service, it is obvious that the sermon must also be in tune with our "storied" nature as human beings. If it is true that we just generally make sense out of life not in intellectual ways first of all but more in narrative ways, then sermons that approach everything in a primarily intellectual manner and that are long on description and short on narrative vividness (long on what we will call "tell" and short on "show," as detailed in chapter 1) will cause people over time to sense a profound disconnect between the preaching moment and the way most of life presents itself the rest of the week. As Smith puts it,

> Our action emerges from how we *imagine* the world. What we do is driven by who we are, by the kind of person we have become. And that shaping of our character is, to a great extent, the effect of stories that have captivated us, that have sunk into our bones—stories that "picture" what we think life is about, what constitutes "the good life." We live *into* the stories we've absorbed; we become characters in the drama that has captivated us.[7]

By way of counterexample to the way most of us operate in life, Smith presents the real-life case of Schneider, a brain-damaged man whose injury rendered him unable to process the world in narrative, storied ways as the rest of us (mostly unconsciously but nonetheless routinely) do. In his damaged state, Schneider was unable to understand even stories that were directly told to him. He could hear and comprehend each detail, but only in a facts-only, intellectual way that rendered him incapable of being moved or delighted or shocked by a story. To Schneider stories were just sequences of facts to be noted and then, as it were, filed away. It is as though when hearing a piano piece played, Schneider is able to pick out and listen to every single note but can never hear a tune that he could remember later and so hum to himself. Drawing on the work of the French phenomenologist Maurice Merleau-Ponty, Smith observes,

[Schneider] is unable to understand the "sense" of a story because he is *only* able to analyze it and process it intellectually. He lacks the narrative sense that affectively "understands" a story, and thus is unable to appreciate the distinctive force and truth of a story that exceeds and eludes the analysis of content. . . . There is an irreducibility to stories that can only be grasped by the imagination—but that is precisely what Schneider lacks.[8]

Most people, upon meeting up with or reading about someone like Schneider, recognize by way of his counterexample the vital role that narrative plays in the ordinary functioning of all of us every day. Yet so very often in the church preachers address people in terms Schneider could understand: rational, didactic, "just the facts, ma'am" messages filled with information and conceptual data but not with narrative. But precisely because we are "storied animals," even the Bible addresses us as such. As Thomas G. Long notes in his book *Preaching and the Literary Forms of the Bible*, a lot of people seem to have this idea that the Bible is a long compendium of doctrines and concepts related to God and to salvation but along the way—here and there in scripture—the Bible throws in stories for illustrative effect.

But that, Long contends, has it just backward: scripture is actually nothing *but* one big story loaded with a myriad of subnarratives, and it is only *out of* those stories—as well as the big story to which they contribute—that the church has deduced and formed doctrines and ideas about God. "In the Bible, narrative is not a device, it is an expression of the way things are."[9] Here again is why those who claim that preachers get in the Bible's way by weaving in vivid stories are wrong. The Bible *itself* authorizes and reveals our need for narrative. To God, reality is one big story in which all of our individual stories find their place. Preachers who cannot tap into this fundamental reality through the use of reality-based stories that both reflect reality and help us imagine that reality in kingdom terms (to evoke Smith's project on "imagining the kingdom") will not address their listeners in anything approaching a holistic way, nor a way that is likely to move them and change them in fundamental ways. A key extension of Long's insight—and this now captures Smith's work as well as the work of narrative theologians like Crites and Root, as summarized above—is that our having been created in the image of God tells us biblically and theologically where our human need for story comes from: it comes from our being made in ways that are fiercely reminiscent of our creator. Our sense of God's living presence in our lives is enhanced through reality-based stories in preaching because God *created* us to perceive him in just this manner.

Narrative Sources

Given this fact, the next question—and it is a difficult one—is how do preachers *find* the stories that matter, stories that will accomplish some of this inside of the preaching moment? Of course, in one sense some might claim that it's never been easier for preachers to find illustrative material—including stories—because what else is Google for? Or, just visit any one of the vast clearinghouses of sermon ideas that can be searched on lots of websites devoted to nothing other than giving preachers that illustrative boost they are seeking for next Sunday.

Although that may seem like an easy, ready-to-hand way to bring more reality into preaching, I would contend that the kind of tailored, contrived, and canned stories/illustrations the preacher is likely to find in A–Z listings on such websites risks adding an air of *un*-reality to many sermons. Our tendency when listening to (or reading) a sermon is to switch off—to become less engaged instead of more engaged—when we hear stories or illustrations that begin with "There once was a man . . ." or with "Someone somewhere once said . . ." Such lines are tip-offs that what is coming next was not discovered by the preacher in the context of real life or from a piece of art (a novel, a film, a journalism article) that did the hard work of depicting real life in compelling ways. No, what is coming next is quite probably a made-up vignette that won't feel true to most people's experiences in life. Too many stories told in sermons are predictably set up to make a certain outcome (and the moral lesson it is supposed to teach) inevitable. But for that very reason such a contrived tale may seem unconvincing.

Real stories work. Real human beings process reality in narrative terms, such that stories in sermons that reflect the lives we all lead in this world will resonate with people at a very deep, basic level. In some ways, as noted above, this observation is the simple part of this project. Even if readers of this volume agree with everything I have claimed here, they know full well that what comes next is actually the difficult part, and that is *finding* good and real stories that will connect with people in the ways just suggested.

It is difficult work but it is not impossible work. As will be suggested in this book, through diligence and through the cultivation of certain habits, the thoughtful preacher can and will over time begin gathering up reality-based stories that will resonate with—and just so, matter to—the people who listen to sermons. Preachers need to know how to collect good stories, but they also need to know the categories of stories that work best for preaching.

As we explore this in what follows, we will begin with a brief review of why "showing" people a given idea or truth in action typically means more than just describing it or "telling" people about it. We will begin, in other words, with the "Why?" of stories in sermons. Why are listeners more engaged with "show" than with just long, discursive sections of "tell"? Why is this principle so vital for all those who write stories and why is it just as vital for preachers to utilize in sermons? Then, having established the "Why?" of narrative, we will move on to two broad applications of the "What?" of sermonic stories. What do preachers need to *show* instead of just *tell*? To answer this question we will explore first how and why certain stories reveal human need, or what Paul Scott Wilson has called the "trouble" of life in this world into which the gospel can and must speak a calming word of peace. But if preachers become adept at finding stories that describe such need, they need secondly to become equally skilled at finding stories that reveal what Wilson calls "grace," which could also be called the gospel in action today.[10] If you *tell* me that God is active today and that Jesus lives and walks with me and talks with me along life's narrow way, my pulse might quicken. It might. But if you can *show* me where God is and what Jesus is doing and how I might come to recognize that gracious activity in the course of one of my average kinetic weeks of soccer practices, piano lessons, and work, well then not only will my pulse certainly quicken, I may find myself offering up prayers of thanksgiving for what I am seeing and experiencing by God's grace.

In the upcoming pages I will detail the role that stories play in sermons and then also provide illustrations of what such stories look like, via excerpts from some of my past sermons and via a recounting of good stories I have found in movies, novels, the news, and more. The goal in this volume is not merely to provide a laundry list of examples—because that would have limited usefulness or appeal—but rather to establish as a principle of preaching the need for all preachers to think pastorally into people's real lives in the crafting of sermons. The goal is to preach sermons that will have real-world traction for those who listen. Finding apt stories is not finally a way for the preacher to show off how well versed he or she is in literature, film, or current events, nor is it merely a way to keep sermons from being boring by livening them up with a spicy story or two. No, finding and presenting stories that matter is ultimately an act of pastoral care and of pastoral love for people who come to church needing to know that their pastor has some sense for what they face day in and day out and that the pastor has also sought a way to find the grace of God active in the midst of all that brokenness. It is also an act of outreach to all who might be in church for the first time on any given Sunday or who have been dabbling in coming to church in recent weeks. These people, too, need to have a sense of reality permeating the worship service, because something about their own day-to-day reality is what has driven them to seek a more active spirituality in their lives in the first place.

As we proceed in the pages ahead, we will return again and again to the narrative nature of our lives, to the idea just mentioned that we are finally storied animals. God has a grand story of which we are privileged by grace to be a part. Preaching seeks miniversions of that narrative to keep listeners tethered to God's story by finding stories that matter and that can become, just so, tools in the hands of the Spirit to apply the gospel to people's hearts.

At one point in the novel *The Great Gatsby*, a character utters an observation along the lines of, "It was all true and it didn't matter." It is a devastating line in that novel's story, but a friend of mine has been known to apply this to some sermons he's heard and in that context, it is devastating indeed. Yet it is the case that I've heard and read very few sermons about which I could not say that the content of the sermon was true. Even quite bad sermons are seldom heretical. But does the sermon's truth *matter*? Is it rooted in a reality to which the listeners can relate? If we are celebrating the great and wonderful grace and the living presence of God in our lives, are we equipping people to join in on that celebration by helping them to know such grace when they see it while sitting at their desk, working in their shop, driving down the highway?

Sermons need more reality, more of real life, in them. And that just makes sense: the gospel and the kingdom of grace it proclaims are, after all, the deepest Reality we know.

Chapter One
Show, Don't Tell

I n past years my wife attended some summer seminars at the Writer's Workshop sponsored by the University of Iowa. These conferences are attended mostly by aspiring novelists who want to learn from the pros what makes for good writing—the kind of writing that would help each such would-be novelist achieve the dream of getting an acceptance letter from a publisher one day. One year my wife returned home sporting a new t-shirt she had bought at the University of Iowa's bookstore. The shirt was emblazoned with a slogan that is trumpeted with regularity at novel-writing seminars: "Show, Don't Tell." Of all the skills aspiring writers of fiction need to learn, "Show, Don't Tell" is touted by the experts as one of the more important writing components to master.

Preachers do not write fiction or novels, of course. Sermons represent a literary form that can be readily distinguished from any number of other writing genres, including novels and short stories. But preachers can nevertheless learn a lot about how to compose compelling sermons by paying attention to the conventions of good writing in other literary forms. Of all the techniques preachers could pick up from writers of fiction, "Show, Don't Tell" may be one of the most vital. Since this is a book about how to weave narrative reality into sermons—and since those stories will usually enliven the power of a sermon to take root in people's lives precisely because they are examples of showing over against telling—it makes sense at the outset to devote some space in this volume to this part of the literary (and of the preaching) craft.

As noted in the introduction, however, there are skeptics out there who doubt that preachers need to learn this technique. Some have grown up hearing so many sermons that were essentially discursive lectures on doctrine—all tell and no show—that they cannot conceive of preaching any other way. Innovations like this whole "Show, Don't Tell" facet to writing look like foreign intrusions into sermons that just possibly the Holy Spirit does not need. But the lack of this in past homiletical practices is no reason to conclude we preachers cannot still learn to become better communicators in the future. If God created us in the unity of our being to be narrative animals, then "Show, Don't Tell" has much to offer the preacher after all.

When experienced writers talk about showing versus telling, they are describing a writing practice that at once makes for more interesting reading and that at the same time conveys information in a manner that will stick with the reader for much longer. The author Ron Rozelle, for instance, points out that by the time you finish reading Harper Lee's Pulitzer Prize–winning novel *To Kill a Mockingbird*, one thing that you as a reader are convinced of as much as anything else is that this novel's hero, Atticus Finch, is the epitome of a good man. Atticus Finch is the embodiment of goodness. But as Rozelle notes, not once in the course of that entire novel do you ever encounter the line "Atticus was a good man." Harper Lee never once *told* her readers that Atticus was good. Instead, in scene after scene, Lee *showed* her readers this man's goodness in ways that are indelible.[1]

Showing through Details

My favorite scene from both the novel and from the film version of *To Kill a Mockingbird* demonstrates this principle of "Show, Don't Tell" in ways that are properly instructive for preachers. It is also a fine example that good storytelling comes from the details that get included. In the story, Atticus Finch is an attorney who nobly defends the wrongly accused black man, Tom Robinson, against the charge of having molested and raped a white woman. Despite Atticus's having mounted a credible case to demonstrate Tom Robinson's innocence, the all-white jury finds Robinson guilty anyway. From the courtroom balcony, Finch's children, Jem and Jean Louise (or "Scout"), had been watching the proceedings among a great crowd of black people who had come to see the trial but who were segregated from sitting on the lower level. After the guilty verdict is announced and the court begins to clear, Harper Lee wrote the following in the narrative voice of the daughter, Jean Louise/Scout:

> Dimly, I saw Atticus pushing papers from the table into his briefcase. He snapped it shut, went to the court reporter and said something, nodded to Mr. Gilmer, and then went to Tom Robinson and whispered something to him. Atticus put his hand on Tom's shoulder as he whispered. Atticus took his coat off the back of his chair and pulled it over his shoulder. Then he left the courtroom, but not by his usual exit. He must have wanted to go home the short way, because he walked quickly down the middle aisle toward the south exit. I followed the top of his head as he made his way to the door. He did not look up. Someone was punching me, but I was reluctant to take my eyes from the people below us, and from the image of Atticus's lonely walk down the aisle.
>
> "Miss Jean Louise?"
>
> I looked around. They were standing. All around us and in the balcony on the opposite wall, the Negroes were getting to their feet. Reverend Sykes's voice was as distant as Judge Taylor's:
>
> "Miss Jean Louise, stand up. Your father's passin.'"[2]

This scene shows us the goodness of Atticus Finch—and the respect it garnered for him among the downtrodden people whom he served—in a way vastly more memorable and more meaningful than if Lee had written at any point in her novel, "Atticus Finch was a good man." But of course, that is but one such scene throughout the novel that shows what goodness looks like in action, even if the trait of goodness is never once singled out for theoretical consideration. As Rozelle points out, it would surely be much more expedient to write, "Atticus Finch was a good man," as opposed to the scene just quoted, which requires many more words and takes up considerably more space on a page. But it is precisely the level of detail and the grain of real life that is experienced in the longer scene that makes goodness vivid.

Preachers take note! A few well-chosen narrative details deliver the freight of what needs to be conveyed better than dozens of abstract words or descriptions ever could. Of course, a novel and a sermon are two very different kinds of writing, but the underlying principle here applies to preaching as well as to novel writing: people learn best not primarily when something is explained to them, but when, through the inclusion of detail and elements of everyday life, people *recognize* in a narrative way truths that resonate with their experience.

If you know someone in real life similar to Atticus Finch, then when you talk about that person to someone else, you also will reach for stories, vignettes, and details that show this person's goodness in action. Indeed, if you were merely to say to someone, "My friend Jane Hogan is a good person," the average person would likely respond, "What do you mean by 'good'? How so?" The answer to such a logical question will inevitably lead to stories chock-full of real-world details that will flesh out Jane's goodness.

Sermons do not exist merely to tell stories, nor do they move along only the way a novel would proceed. But whenever sermons talk about scenarios of real life, just *telling* people that scenario X exists in the world will never be as effective as *showing* one clear and detailed example of that scenario in action. And please notice: if just mentioning Jane's "goodness" in the abstract would not be enough to satisfy a conversation partner on a Tuesday morning over coffee, then it will not be acceptable on a Sunday morning when talking about the goodness of God. When the preacher says, "My Savior is a good person," those listening will respond in their hearts, "What do you mean by 'good'? How so?"

The writer John Gardener once noted, "Detail is the lifeblood of fiction."

> Instead of writing "She felt terrible," [the writer] can show—by the precise gesture or look or by capturing the character's exact turn of phrase—subtle nuances of the character's feeling. The more abstract a piece of writing is, the less vivid the dream it sets off in the reader's mind. One can feel happy or bored or cross in a thousand ways: the abstract adjective says almost nothing. The precise gesture nails down the one feeling right for the moment. This is what is meant when writing teachers say that one should "show," not "tell." And this, it should be added, is *all* that the writing teacher means. Good writers may "tell" about almost anything in fiction except the characters' feelings. One may tell the reader that the character went to a private school . . . or one may tell the reader that the character hates spaghetti; but with rare exceptions the characters' feelings must be demonstrated: fear, love, excitement, doubt, embarrassment, despair become real only when they take the form of events—action (or gesture), dialogue, or physical reaction to setting.[3]

The details flesh out an idea or a circumstance in a way straightforward, linear descriptions cannot accomplish. Details put us viscerally in touch with circumstances and situations we all experience every week. The novelist Francine Prose once quoted a friend who teaches creative writing as saying, "'Trust me on this,' my friend said, 'God really is in the details.' If God is in the details, we must all on some deep level believe that the truth is in there too, or maybe it is that God is truth: Details are what persuade us that someone is telling the truth—a fact that every liar knows instinctively and too well."[4] Prose goes on to quote the philosopher and theologian Alfred North Whitehead, who observed, "We think in generalities. But we live in detail."[5]

5

The Bible as Source for "Show, Don't Tell"

But this facet of the writing craft that pays such careful attention to the grain of real life through the inclusion of vivid and specific details is found not just in contemporary fiction: it is on display in also some of the most memorable parts of the Bible. Think of Jesus's landmark parables of the good Samaritan and the prodigal son. Today *we* label the former parable "the *good* Samaritan," but like Harper Lee with Atticus Finch, the truth is that in his telling of the parable as reported by Luke, Jesus never once *tells* us that the Samaritan is good, but just asks, "Which of those three, do you think, was a neighbor?" Later Bible editors added subheadings like "the good Samaritan" because they, too, caught what Jesus was *showing*.

The father of the prodigal in Luke 15 is likewise known to Christians everywhere as a loving and gracious man, even though Jesus never once told his listeners that this was the case. In his parables, although Jesus was not adverse to telling us information here and there, mostly Jesus is a paragon of "Show, Don't Tell" by allowing some of the most important parts of his stories, parables, and sermons to emerge, not through brief descriptive sentences that hit us over the head by telling us something obvious, but through our seeing the characters in action. Along the lines of what John Gardner noted, Jesus in Luke 15 also never tells us that the father was overjoyed, happy, or giddy at his lost son's return. But only a fool could fail to notice that every single one of those emotions was present in the father's heart. You could see it in his actions and hear it in how he later defended those actions to his upset older son. In the introduction I asserted that what good stories really do in preaching is bring us into contact with the living presence of God in our lives. That's what Jesus did, too: he did not tell people *about* the God he called his Father but brought his listeners into living contact with that God.

When this is done well in writing and in storytelling generally, descriptive "tell" sentences either before or (most certainly) after the

6

story actually become superfluous and even clunky. Writer Nancy Kress counsels aspiring novelists and even experienced writers to beware, therefore, of the tendency to overexplain or to ruin a well-constructed "show" section by giving in to the temptation to "tell" what it all means after all. "Ironically most writers tell after they show not because they mistrust the reader's intelligence to 'get' the point, but rather because they lack faith in their own prose."[6]

To connect this to what was just observed about Jesus' own parables, it is not difficult to perceive how ham-fisted it would have been of our Lord—or of Luke in reporting the parable—to tack on after the parable's final words something like, "And so we see, beloved, that the father was loving, the younger son was repentant, and the older son was a bit of an entitled twerp. And remember, too, that I told this parable and those other two about the sheep and the coin because, you see, I am trying to give some hope to these 'sinners' sitting in front of me whose presence upset the twerpy Pharisees who, just so you know, are represented in this last parable by the older brother who just cannot generate any joy over the fact that sometimes the lost come home, which in this case I should point out is not really some person's literal home but by 'home' I mean the kingdom of God . . ."

This is *not* the word of the Lord.

Thanks be to God!

Jesus typically did not tack on such long "tell" sections. Alas, very often preachers conclude their stories or their sermons by doing precisely this. To the minds of some people—both those who preach sermons but also to the minds of not a few people who listen to sermons (and that is probably because they have been trained to listen for all the wrong things)—it's just not a sermon until or unless there are long stretches of didactic teaching and linear descriptions, all capped off with a heaping helping of moralizing, in which listeners are told not just what it all means but what they must now go out and accomplish on account of what it all means.

More often than not, however, what we preachers struggle with is not yielding to the temptation to mess up our fine "show" sections with unnecessary "tell" sentences but rather the struggle is to remember to include "show" sections in our sermons to begin with. Left to our own devices, many of us tend to have a default setting of writing and preaching sermons that are exceedingly long on "tell" but very, very short on "show." In some ways, this is a hazard of seminary training, where in typical academic fashion we are required to write essays and formal papers that are chock-full of "tell," but that pass muster with professors just fine, even if those writings display very little by way of "show." That works in academic discourse but not so well in pulpit speech.

Balancing Tell with Show

But before we consider other reasons why we preachers tend to do this—and see some examples of this tendency—it needs to be noted that nothing in what we are considering here is meant to convey the notion that sermons may never "tell." Sermons, as a matter of fact, absolutely need to have a decent amount of "tell" in them because all sermons include a significant teaching component. Mostly what preachers teach and tell the congregation about is the meaning of the scripture passage on which that particular sermon is based or perhaps necessary definitions of various doctrines or theological terms or the meaning of this or that fruit of the Spirit.

The linear and "tell" parts of the sermon are the necessary parts of the sermon in which information is conveyed: What is the setting of this Bible text, where does it fit inside the larger book or epistle of which this text is a part, where does it fit inside the larger witness of scripture and of salvation history, what do the various words and phrases in the text mean? If a preacher wants the congregation to come away from a given sermon understanding some important elements of Mark's Gospel (and how those elements are on display in the passage under consideration that week), then those thematic and literary elements will need to be explained, detailed, laid out before the people in a fairly systematic way. Also, for the simple sake of clarity, at many points in sermons the preacher will need to label some phenomenon, some spiritual discipline, some practice of piety and define what each such item is. At times it's important to point out for the congregation the difference between the gifts of the Spirit and the fruit of the Spirit, and there may well be no better way to do that than by *telling* people the differences. All good sermons help to answer such vital questions about the text at hand, and doing this requires sections of "tell" in the form of straightforward descriptions.

There is, of course, nothing wrong with that. As John Gardener points out, novelists do their fair share of telling inside the story. But then the telling is inside the larger story, not outside of the narrative or disconnected from it. Ron Rozelle gives the following example from Masuji Ibuse's novel *Black Rain* that involves the dropping of the atomic bomb on the Japanese city of Hiroshima. Nowhere in this novel does Ibuse write the line, "The city suffered great damage in the blast." Instead, at one point Ibuse wrote the following passage that displays a beautiful way of telling inside the story:

> Among the ruins, the reflection of the sun on the pieces of broken glass on the road was so strong that it was difficult to hold your head up as you walked. The smell of death was a little fainter than the day before, but the places where houses had collapsed into tile-covered heaps stank vilely and were covered with great, black swarms of flies. The relief squads clearing the ruins seemed to have been joined by reinforcements since I saw some men whose clothes, though bleached with frequent washing, were not soiled with sweat and grime as yet.[7]

As Rozelle goes on to note, the longer paragraph is better than the one sentence, "The city suffered great damage in the blast," not only because, as noted above, the longer passage is rich with details, but also because it draws you in more as a reader—senses are engaged, memories of similar scenes that were encountered in person are stirred. But then Rozelle says, "The longer version is not better because it is all showing and no telling. It's better because it is *both* showing and telling. Your fiction has to be a balanced blend of both approaches."[8] It is similar in preaching, and as we will see below, a good sermon will contain a kind of rhythm between telling and showing. But never is this "both/and" approach to telling and showing more important to include in a sermon than in those passages that make perhaps the sermon's most vital point as to what the entire message means, in the context of people's real lives out in the world Monday through Saturday every week.

Examples of Moving from Tell to Show

Perhaps due to having themselves heard so many sermons across the years that were all "tell" and no "show"—or perhaps because it is frankly easier to "tell" than to "show"—preachers often fail to balance out their telling with vivid, detailed, and specific sections of the all-important showing of what the sermon is talking about. Since it would be oddly ironic in this chapter if we were to continue to discuss this in "tell" terms rather than "show" terms, it makes sense to get specific by showing some concrete examples of what this looks like in actual sermons.

Consider the following paragraphs, which represent a kind of distillation of several student sermons I received in a class a few semesters back:

> The psalmist ends with a call to all people: "Blessed are people whose God is the LORD." Indeed. The people who are in God's hands are truly blessed. They are blessed because they are the ones who have the Lord of creation on their side. In their corner is the one who causes mountains to smoke and waters to surge. The God who routs enemies is the also the God who blesses them. The psalmist reminds the reader that if they place their trust in this God, then this protection and blessing can be theirs.

And the same holds true for us today. We currently have the same access to the hands of God the warrior. God will fight for us today. Perhaps his fighting will not be as dramatic as loosing lightning bolts at our enemies, but he will fight nonetheless. When Jesus gave his disciples the Lord's Prayer, he told them to ask God to "deliver us from evil."

God will help us fight the battles against ourselves. God desires to keep us from falling into temptation. If we call on the name of the Lord, he will help us overcome our shortcomings. God again and again promises that he will give us the strength to battle adversity if we only put our trust in him. On our own we are slaves to sin, but with God we are entitled to freedom. On our own righteousness is impossible; through God all things are possible.

All by themselves, these paragraphs convey a lot of important and utterly true information. On its own level, the kind of material presented here is engaging and interesting too. It's all true but . . . does it matter? The preacher is telling the congregation many things: a mighty God is in our corner and is on our side; God still fights for God's people today; God helps us in battles with even our own sinful impulses in moments of temptation; God turns us from slaves to sin into righteous people after all.

The difficulty with the paragraphs above is this is where the typical preacher stops (even as this is where my students usually stop). We are told *that* God does all these wonderful things, but we are not given a single hint that could *show* us when and where this happens today and how any given listener would be able to recognize this divine activity in his or her life should the listener encounter this set of divine actions in the upcoming week. In other words, this is the equivalent of Harper Lee's writing only "Atticus Finch was a good man" but never including a scene like the courtroom narrative quoted above.

Good sermon listeners cry out for more "show" and less "tell." If God is not literally loosing lightning bolts today as part of his warrior efforts on our behalf, what is God doing instead? How will we know it if we see it? When will we know when to celebrate this in loud songs of praise? Can the preacher utilize enough imagination and invoke enough of the preacher's own careful thought and study on these matters to name even one contemporary battlefield on which God fights for God's people? Can we hear one story about an actual, specific temptation in someone's life that God helped the person overcome, and can we then further see just how that worked out and what this involved? Until and unless preachers can introduce stories and images and illustrations that are true to life in fleshing all this out, even the grandest of biblical and theological truths may not move beyond the point of being just ideas and concepts floating in the air of the sanctuary, failing to accomplish what needs to be accomplished, which is bringing people into living contact with the living God who really is an active presence and force in our world and in our lives.

Here is another example that I complied from some sermons based on Psalm 8:

> It's similar for us today. God has not only created us a little lower than the heavenly beings but he has even crowned us with glory and honor. That isn't a picture that translates very easily into our culture—being crowned with glory and honor—so some of you might be wondering, "What does it mean that we are crowned by God with glory?" It seems to me that the glory of humanity and that which gives us honor above all other creatures is that we are included in God's plan and declared his special part of creation. The response that arises from being crowned with glory and honor is obvious and it is included in Psalm 8. This is our purpose. Everyone wants to know their purpose and it is clearly given by David in Psalm 8.

Here the sermon actually named the very question that thoughtful listeners would, by this point in the sermon, have asked in their hearts: What does it mean to be crowned with glory and honor? How does this translate into our world in the twenty-first century? Good questions. Logical questions. The congregation yearns to hear them answered. But instead of moving beyond just telling us some facts and then raising good questions, once again the sermon stopped here and left the specifics of "glory and honor" undefined, retreating back to a repetition of the very "tell" section that preceded the asking of the listeners' question. But by doubling down on more description, this preacher in no way actually answers the question in ways that would take on flesh for listeners in the week ahead. People here needed to be *shown* what glory and honor are and how both could be on display when a person is working in her shop or sitting in a classroom or driving a truck across the country.

Imagine what a difference it would have made in that Psalm 8 sermon had the preacher inserted something like the following right after asking the question, "What does it mean that we are crowned by God with glory?"

When I think about that glory crown, I remember, along with many of you, our sister Millicent Faber, or "Aunt Millie" as most of us knew her before she died last year. Because Aunt Millie had an eye for the lonely, the marginalized. She could enter a room and spy, within seconds, the person on the fringe. And she'd make her way to that person. She'd smile that warm smile of hers, engage him in conversation, put her hand on the man's shoulder and in all these ways draw him into the center of the fellowship after all. When you were sick, Millie was at the front door with a casserole. When a child was dejected, Millie was there with a twinkle in her eye and a word of encouragement. Whenever I saw Millie breaking away from her friends in the church lobby to reach out to someone sitting by herself, out of the corner of my eye I could see clear as day a crown of glory on Millie's head. As Psalm 8 shows us, the God who is majestic above the heavens has a keen and curious ability to regard little old us on this cosmic speck of real estate called the earth. God sees us in our littleness and neediness and has crowned us with glory and honor to do the same thing for others. Millie knew that, and how well she wore that crown indeed!

The presence of Millie in a sermon like this will do more to help people celebrate and understand a crown of glory than ten more paragraphs of just *telling* about crowns could ever accomplish.

The Challenge of "Show"

As already acknowledged, however, there is a reason why we preachers often stop well short of having good "show" sections, contenting ourselves merely to repeat broad biblical and theological truths: it is far easier to preach that way than doing the hard work of locating specifics. But just those specifics are typically the difference between people's absorbing concepts in their minds and their being able to see God in action in their daily lives.

Additionally, another facet of sermon writing that makes this properly daunting is the fact that the preacher wants to be careful to identify stories or images that are fitting and apt. If the preacher of the sermon that claimed God still fights for us like a warrior wanted to find concrete examples of such divine intervention, what might those examples be? Caution would demand that the preacher not choose something that will come off as politically charged on the one hand or something that seemed merely petty or overly simplified on the other hand. Preachers also do not wish to sketch scenarios that seem fake, canned, or so patently convenient as to come off as decidedly unreal. It can be hard work to find just the right story, but as the balance of this book will argue, not only can this be done, but when preachers actually do the work of looking for and archiving the rights kinds of stories, they will eventually discover a trove of good ideas that are both accessible to the preacher when they are needed and that are fitting for the sermon and the scripture passage in question as well.

"Detail is the lifeblood of fiction," as John Gardner wrote, but detail is no less the lifeblood of preaching. Finding such specific detail so as to weave it into sermons is the key principle and tactic that preachers can and must learn from teachers of writing and from the entire "Show, Don't Tell" school of thought. Earlier in this chapter, it was noted that were someone merely to tell another person, "My friend Jane Hogan is a good person," the follow-up question would be "How so?" But suppose you did ask that of the person who asserted Jane's goodness only to hear the reply, "I dunno. I just think she's good." Not only would such an answer be unsatisfying—and likely lead you to press yet again for some detailed examples of Jane's alleged goodness—but if the other person persisted in a shoulder-shrugging inability to come up with anything concrete, you might well conclude that this person does not finally know what he's talking about. (Worse, you might wonder how "good" Jane is after all, seeing as nothing comes to your friend's mind by way of example.)

It is no different in sermons. If a preacher goes on and on about resisting the false gods of our age but cannot, even when pressed, name even one such false god—much less what form the resisting of this god might take—sooner or later a congregation may conclude that the preacher does not know what she is talking about, and the sermon then becomes a collection of generic truisms that seem unable to live and breathe in the real world. This concept of "Show, Don't Tell" is not, therefore, a way merely to make sermons more *interesting* but is the key principle that helps sermons be more *real*, by virtue of their ability to engage with real-world examples and scenarios the likes of which most people in the congregation encounter during the average week as it is. Of even more vital importance is the fact that it is the living and active presence of God himself that comes into people's lives through the proclamation of God's word and of God's good news. When sermons become more real on account of the specificity that good, thoughtful stories bring, it is no less than *God* who finally becomes more real, entering people's well-defined trouble and answering it with specified grace. As I have said to students who arch their eyebrows in skepticism over the need for life's specifics as laid out in a good story, if you cannot get away with such a lack of specificity anywhere else in life, why should preaching be any different?

Examples of "Show, Don't Tell" in Sermons

What follows are a couple of examples of stories I used in my own sermons in which I tried to balance—to varying degrees of success, no doubt—sermonic "tell" sections with at least one image or story of "show."

The Pastoral Story

Some years ago I was assigned Hebrews 2:1-13 as a preaching text. The sermon ended up centering on the verses in that passage that admit that for now and in this challenging world, it is often difficult to see the Lordship of Jesus. Yes, we confess that God has (a la Psalm 8) placed everything under Jesus's feet, but the author to the Hebrews is honest enough to admit, "Yet at present, we do not see everything subject to him. But we see Jesus." Somehow, the author asserts, the eyes of faith see the suffering servant Jesus in the midst of this broken world—a world that frankly does not look like it is under the Lordship management of Jesus. In the "tell" section of this sermon I pointed out how the author developed these ideas and what a clarion gospel claim it was when the author slipped in those words, "But we see Jesus." After that the sermon proceeded as follows:

> The preacher Tom Long once noted that when leading worship seminars in different parts of the country, he often meets up with people whose number one complaint about worship has nothing to do with contemporary music, new hymnals, or bad sermons. Instead Long has heard some people complain that what nettles them the most about worship services are the announcements.

And you know how that goes. You've just come off a rousing rendition of the hymn "Holy, Holy, Holy." The piano and instrumentalists had been playing at a glorious full throttle, the praise team's descant was just perfect, and you felt as though you were winging your way into the very precincts of heaven. Then, soon after the hymn is finished, you hear the pastor say, "Let's remember Beatrice who is back in the hospital with another intestinal blockage." And suddenly heaven seems far away again and earth has made a roaring comeback! Can't we skip the announcements and just focus on stained-glass stuff on Sundays?

No. Because as Tom Long went on to note, such things belong in worship, assuming, that is, we want people to see the real Jesus to whom this real world is subject in its every detail. We need to see Jesus's connection to hospitals and surgeries and sadness because those are precisely the situations in which people need to receive the grace that lets them see Jesus.

In one of his fine sermons, Fred Craddock notes that the disciples-turned-apostles performed what Craddock calls a majestic flip-flop. You see, all along the Jews, who were waiting for the Messiah, summed up their anticipation with the phrase, "When the Messiah comes, no suffering." "See that person over there all shriveled up with arthritis and in constant pain? Well, when the Messiah comes, you won't see that anymore. When the Messiah comes, no suffering. See that blind man? See that crippled woman? See that broken family? Well, when the Messiah comes, you won't see that again. When the Messiah comes, no suffering." But for the disciples-turned-apostles who ended up meeting the real Messiah in Jesus of Nazareth, the Crucified One, they ended up doing a flip-flop, a reversal, as they ended up proclaiming that for now and until he comes again, wherever there is suffering, that's where you will find the Messiah!

In my pastoral care class back in seminary, we had a guest one day who was a hospital chaplain who specialized in working with sick and dying children. She told us several stories, one of which was about a little boy, perhaps six or seven, who had end-stage leukemia. In what proved to be his last week of life in the hospital, the little boy had no small measure of pain, which apparently caused some hallucinations. Several times the little boy saw a strange man passing by the doorway to his room, causing the tyke some alarm, which required his mother's reassurance. One afternoon, as the mother cradled her mortally ill child in her arms, the little boy's body stiffened as he again cried out, "That man is back, Mommy!" The mother was about to reassure him yet again when suddenly his thin body relaxed. The boy looked his mother in the eye and with a smile said, "Oh, Mommy! I didn't recognize him, but it's Jesus! I have to go now." And with great peace he died.

At present we do not see everything subject to him. No, we sure don't, not in this world of leukemia and war and sorrow and pity. But by faith we see Jesus. What a grace God has given to us, that we receive fresh glimpses of Jesus, even right in the middle of life's hard knocks and outright tragedies. God gives us enough faith, enough grace, to see the truth of what Jesus has done. And by grace, it's enough. We can go on.

As stories go, this one is admittedly dramatic and unusual. But my hope was that it locates this "seeing Jesus" idea in a real-life situation that *shows* what seeing Jesus in the midst of brokenness can be like in a way my merely describing it and telling about it could never do. Even as I encountered this story in the midst of a seminary class, preachers will discover and hear stories like this—some less dramatic but no less poignant—in the course of ministry and life experience. Weaving them into sermons shows the congregation the truth about Jesus's presence in our world and in our lives in a way far more indelible than repeated assertions of that truth could ever do. The reason people are more likely to remember this story is not just because it is dramatic or emotionally loaded—though let's admit that this story has plenty of drama and emotion—but mainly because, as we noted in the introduction, story and narrative are the way we parse our lives just generally. Such a story connects listeners powerfully with the presence of Christ in our world and in our lives in ways that are emotionally indelible. Preachers ignore that fact to their peril.

The Grain of Everyday Life

In a sermon on Matthew 6 some years ago, the message pondered the juxtaposition between Jesus's lovely call for us to "seek first the kingdom" with his startling concluding words in that same passage to the effect that "each day has enough trouble of its own." Similar to the Hebrews 2 passage, here Jesus is realistic enough to know that seeking the kingdom in this trouble-filled world will not be easy. Nonetheless, this is what we are called by grace to do. Reflecting on what this might mean in our daily lives—and again, following a "tell" section of the sermon in which I explained why Jesus combined kingdom seeking with an admission about daily troubles—the sermon concluded,

> In his commentary on this passage, Dale Bruner is at his lyric best when he invites us to see our daily actions as spiritual after all. On any given day we have to do the laundry, brush our child's hair, attend committee meetings, spend time talking on the phone to someone whom we love just fine, but whose call to us did not come at the most opportune moment we could think of. And so we start to think that surely a "spiritual" life must include better, other, more obviously pious acts than these.

> But perhaps not, Bruner says. When we do our work well, when we attend even the most routine of committee meetings, we are contributing to the functioning of God's world and become, just so, agents of God's providential care of society. When we talk with a friend on the phone, we may be providing love and compassion—a mercy that may be needed by this dear soul at that particular moment. Indeed, sometimes we are at our most Christlike precisely in the interruptions that come. Maybe ministry is just generally what happens in life's interrupted moments.[9]

> Taking time to brush my child's hair may seem at times to take me away from more "important" matters, but what if I view it instead as a precious moment to be with my child, perhaps as one of the few times all day I'll get to touch him and look at him. Maybe the reason we are told that God has the hairs of our heads numbered is because God takes joy in being able to stare at our

heads with the tender affection of a Father for his child. When God "brushes" our hair, God does so lovingly, counting the hairs as he goes and delighting in just being with us. "Seek first the kingdom," Jesus said. But we don't need to go looking for that reign of God—it is already present in the most ordinary things we do if only we do them in the name of Christ.

In her wonderful novel, *Gilead*, Marilynne Robinson uses the character of Rev. John Ames to model one of the deepest insights Robinson said she gleaned from her study of John Calvin: being fully present in the moment. Rev. Ames, as he nears the end of his life and as he basks in having a young son born late in his life, is often making observations like this one. Rev. Ames is in his upstairs study when he observes the following:

"I saw a bubble float past my window, fat and wobbly and ripening toward that dragonfly blue they turn just before they burst. So I looked down at the yard and there you were, you and your mother, blowing bubbles at the cat, such a barrage of them that the poor beast was beside herself at the glut of opportunity. She was actually leaping into the air, our insouciant Soapy! Some of the bubbles drifted up through the branches, even above the trees. You two were too intent on the cat to see the celestial consequences of your worldly endeavors. They were very lovely. Your mother is wearing her blue dress and you are wearing your red shirt and you were kneeling on the ground together with Soapy between and that effulgence of bubbles rising, and so much laughter. Ah, this life, this world."[10]

In this brilliant passage the kingdom of God is seen shimmering in a soap bubble, in the leaping of a cat, in the laughter of a little boy and his mother. "Seek first the kingdom," Jesus says. And so we do. In our every mundane act on a Tuesday or a Thursday, in our every prayer that emerges from the midst of our troubled lives and our troubled, troubling world, we seek the kingdom. "Each day has enough trouble of its own," Jesus said. That's why we pray. But in so praying, we find another truth: each day has a lot of the kingdom in it, too. When we view life that way, we won't worry about tomorrow. We will be too busy rejoicing in what God has already given *today*.

Brushing a child's hair, attending committee meetings, playing with soap bubbles and cats: these details are intended to pick up some of the grain of everyday real life in a way similar to the advice for would-be novelists that was noted above. Detail is the lifeblood of fiction, as John Gardener put it, but it pumps a whole lot of life into sermons, too. In that sermon, I could have told the congregation until I was blue in the face—or until they were blue in the face listening to me!—that the kingdom is everywhere. But thanks to the good commentary work of Frederick Dale Bruner, the everyday activity of hair-brushing got into this sermon in a way that may well have led many listeners to think about the kingdom of God probably the very next morning when brushing a little girl's hair in the bathroom before she trudged off to another day of second grade. When preachers talk about the need to ponder the power of "show" to follow up on a sermon's "tell" sections, this is exactly what is meant, and it is the kind of practical, everyday application of the gospel that is sought by all who preach sermons and most certainly by those who listen to sermons as well.

Keeping It Vivid

Before we leave this consideration of "Show, Don't Tell," we will ponder a few rhetorical techniques pastors can utilize so as to make even more vivid and compelling the stories that are told in sermons. This will certainly not be an exhaustive list of ways to tell stories well but presents at least some initial ideas for preachers to keep in mind. As with the earlier material here in this book, the point is how to connect the way we communicate in most of life with the way we communicate in the pulpit.

First-Person Speech

First, a basic technique that will help preachers weave more reality-based narrative into preaching is a simple reminder to speak in the first person. As I often say to students, if I were to go to the student center on any given day during lunchtime and eavesdrop on the conversations going on, I know to a very high degree of certainty that with great regularity I would hear things such as, "So I was sitting at breakfast this morning gnawing on my bagel when my wife looked up from peering into the fridge and said to me, 'George, you polished off the orange juice again, didn't you, and then didn't put it on the grocery list! You know, honey, sometimes you can be a real galoot!'"

This is what we do when swapping stories over something like a lunch table: we do not merely *report* on conversations we've had with other people, we *reconstruct* them, we speak in the voices of the people who are included in the story. What's more, the way we quote a given person and the intonations of voice we ourselves adopt in imitating him or her tell our listeners everything they need to know in terms of what the other person's attitude was. If you are the person at lunch relating such a breakfast encounter with your wife, your tone of voice in repeating what your wife said will render it unnecessary for you then to say to your friends, "You see, she was upset with me and out of patience." When you tell a story well and reconstruct what the other person said to you, there will be no need to say something so obvious: the people to whom you are telling this story already "got it" just from how you quoted this other person.

Yet as I also say to my students, the fact that I would hear such things over and over again in the student center makes it the more amazing to me as a teacher when these same students get into a pulpit to preach a sermon and yet never speak in the first person when telling stories or retelling Bible stories. For some reason, in sermons we shut down our natural tendency to reconstruct conversations in favor of just reporting on them. We tell instead of show. For instance, in Mark 8, after Jesus predicts his upcoming suffering and death, Mark tells us that Peter pulled Jesus aside to say, "God forbid that any of that should ever happen to you." In a sermon, that exact line from Peter could be quoted in Peter's voice when the preacher sum-marizes and retells that part of the narrative.

Or the preacher could even embellish it a bit: "At this point Peter draped his arm across Jesus's shoulders, pulled him aside the way a coach might huddle with one of his players, and said, 'Now, now, Jesus, let's have no more of this defeatist talk! If you keep talking this way, you're going to discourage us. No one likes a downer, Lord!'" That would be a vivid way to let the color of the narrative enter into the sermon. The preacher could also use vocal intonations that would convey Peter's condescending attitude in calling Jesus out for what Peter clearly perceived to be some very bad theology on Jesus's part. Yet again and again we have all heard sermons in which instead of speaking in the first person, the preacher instead rather dryly says, "At this point Peter informed Jesus that he did not want to hear such things from Jesus." Well, yes, that is true and definitely conveys the thrust of that part of Mark 8, but it does so in ways that are vastly less vivid and interesting for listeners. A good part of showing over against telling in sermons can be accomplished by using first-person speech whenever possible in the telling or retelling of stories.

Be Specific, not General

Second, another storytelling component that preachers naturally include in ordinary conversations but that they sometimes forget to include when writing sermons is *specificity*. In many ways this is of a piece with the earlier observations about including details, though this kind of specificity goes even a bit further in order to create vivid pictures in people's minds. Listeners pay better attention and have images formed much more readily in their minds when specific de-scriptions are given. When telling stories in sermons, therefore, the preacher should never refer merely to "a truck" but to "a beat-up blue Dodge pickup with rust chewing at the rocker panels." If a story involves a couple having dinner at a nice restaurant somewhere, in-stead of referring generically to "food" or to "their dinners," take a big step toward concrete imagery by saying they were eating "a seared strip loin of pork with a side of truffled potatoes and wilted collard greens." Rather than describing something as just being "a nice day," point out that it was "one of those spring days when the sky seemed bluer than usual and when the sunlight lit up those pink dogwood blossoms in ways that gave you a thrill just to look at them." *Be specific!*

Granted, all writers and all preachers need to beware of engaging in overly purple prose, in which the descriptions and adjectives are so abundant and so overwrought as to call attention to themselves in ways that will actually get in the way of the listeners' ability to appreciate the specificity of the descriptions. But even something as simple as saying it was a "sports car" instead of just "a car," or mentioning that the little boy was "freckle-faced" as opposed to just being "a boy," can make a big difference in terms of how vividly a story or a description comes across to those listening to a sermon. Again, when we swap stories with one another over lunch, we take care to mention the make of our automobile, the color of the siding on our house, or what we were eating at the restaurant. The "trick," if you will, is to make sure we do not let this kind of specificity fade away when crafting stories inside a sermon.

Using Imagination

Third, another storytelling feature to note is the prudent and disciplined use of imagination. By the term *imagination* here I do not intend to move in the direction of conjuring imaginary worlds or concocting scenes that have never and may never exist. Rather, *imagination* in this context means the preacher is making use of his or her mind to visualize biblical scenes in ways that go beyond the strict confines of the text's own descriptions but that nevertheless nestle the text into familiar settings that will help bring out the passage's core truth in more vivid, easier-to-recognize ways. But notice that I am careful to qualify this as *prudent and disciplined*: imagination in telling stories or in embellishing Bible stories cannot run wild or be pushed to the breaking point by including elements that some may find absurd or overly colloquial or too cute. When utilized well, however, the preacher's imagination can reframe familiar stories or well-known sayings in ways that will make them feel fresh and new to listeners.

Fred Craddock is a master of this in ways that typically do not call undue attention to such flights of imagination and that weave their way into the sermon quite seamlessly. In a sermon pondering the amazing covenantal promises God made to Abraham and Sarah, for instance, Craddock says that at times it must have seemed simply impossible to Abraham and Sarah that they had somehow become the parents of a people that would one day be as numerous as the stars in the sky and the sands on the seashore. But to drive this home, Craddock threw in some contemporary language, so as to imagine the baby Isaac sitting in his little high chair in Abraham and Sarah's kitchen, his face all smeared with oatmeal and flashing a smile at his parents to show off the handful of teeth he had in his little mouth. Stars in the sky, sands on the seashore . . . from this one little child?

By extension of this basic technique of using the imagination, one could imagine suggesting that if the rich young man were around today, he'd have on a nice Armani suit, his eyes shaded by an expensive-looking pair of Ray-Ban sunglasses. Perhaps the unjust judge in Luke 18 would be annoyed by the persistent widow when she interrupts his tee time at the golf course or his after-work martini at a local lounge with her incessant pleas for justice.

In an updated telling of the Prodigal Son parable, Richard Ward imagined that today the younger son's plight in the far country might involve becoming a dishwasher at a Chicago blues club where after scraping off old rib bones, sloppy coleslaw, and baked beans into a trash can, the boy was so hungry he was tempted to reach down into the trash and eat the leavings of other people's barbeque dinners. Of course, it might also be enough for a preacher to hew closer to the actual text of Luke 15 and say simply that he got so hungry he wanted to eat pig slop. But even then it might be a good idea to remind people who have never seen pig slop exactly what goes into pig slop on traditional pig farms (and by the way, slop includes everything from a farm kitchen that the people did not want to put in their mouths in the first place!).[11]

Hearing the Bible's Stories Afresh

Fourth, yet another place where a disciplined imagination can make stories—again, including even the retelling of the Bible's own stories—come more alive is in the area of conveying not simply *what* was said by a given character in the story but also *how* it may have been said. The Bible generally does not tell its readers the manner in which something was said. Adverbs like *cheerfully*, *mournfully*, or *angrily* rarely accompany phrases like "Jesus said" or "Mary replied." But everything we say conveys some kind of emotion or another, and the things spoken by characters in the Bible were originally spoken in one fashion or another, too. Imaginative preachers will wonder about this and look for clues in the context of a given passage to suggest for a congregation how to perceive the acoustics of what is said. Too often preachers and others who read the Bible treat every utterance of Jesus as being delivered in the exact same tone of voice. (Perhaps this perception was aided and abetted by some of those movies about Jesus in which the actors who portrayed Jesus delivered their every line in a kind of glassy-eyed, otherworldly monotone.) But if Jesus was as human as everyone else and communicated as such, then surely his voice had as many different intonations as anyone else's voice had, and, as is always true, the context in which something is spoken—and also the content of the words themselves—help to determine the specifics of intonation and vocal nuance.

One of my favorite examples of this comes from the opening verses of John 14. Often when these verses are read aloud—and about as often when they are requoted inside a sermon—the words, "Let not your hearts be troubled. Believe in God, believe also in me" are presented as a confident, straightforward utterance whose intonation is not all that different from what you'd expect to hear from someone saying "I'd like a double cheeseburger, medium fries, and a Coke." Jesus thus comes off as colorless and passionless in saying these words about comfort and the many rooms he has prepared for people.

But does the context indicate there could well be another way to hear these word from our Lord? It is, after all, the night in which Jesus will be betrayed. The atmosphere is gloomy, taut. What's more, in the seconds before Jesus spoke his now well-known words in John 14, Judas had just slinked off into the darkness to do his dirty deed even as Jesus had just mournfully had to inform his beloved disciple Peter that within hours, he also would be denying Jesus up and down. Isn't it just possible, therefore, that when Jesus said, "Let not your hearts be troubled . . ." that he did so with a quivering chin, trembling lips, and with tears forming in the corners of his eyes? If a preacher suggested that way of Jesus's speaking these words, the congregation would come to see how these words about not being troubled are needed precisely because—as it was for Jesus, so it is for us—we live in a powerfully troubling world.

The times when we most need to hear Jesus telling us not to have troubled hearts will be when we're at the bedside of a hospice patient about to draw her final breaths on this earth or at the funeral of a child. In those circumstances, most people would not shout Jesus' words in John 14 in triumphant tones or with a kind of matter-of-fact lack of emotion. No, in those troubling times when we most need to hear Jesus tell us not to be finally troubled, our voices break, our emotions are on edge, and how we speak will reflect all that.

Perhaps hearing Jesus say those famous words in the context of his own emotions as they churned in him that particular night will provide just the right acoustics in which some hurting people in a congregation need to receive those words on any given Sunday morning. This is an example of retelling a Bible story well in a sermon, but

27

conveying genuine emotion applies equally well to the first-person speech we use in any story or illustration told in a sermon.

In preaching seminars and in seminary classrooms this idea has generated a lot of hand wringing. Many fear that the preacher could move so far beyond the confines of the biblical text as to *change* that text in ways no preacher should do. And indeed, caution is called for. A preacher may not impute to a certain character in the Bible any random way of speaking a given line that the preacher wants. The context will help determine what the range of possibilities is. Further, even when a preacher opts for one particular way of speaking a character's line, it is best to frame this as, "Perhaps he said it this way," or, "Can we imagine that she may have sounded like this?" It is wiser to signal that this is a *possible* way to hear a given text rather than to claim definitively that the person in question *must* have said it in the way the preacher is suggesting. But even taking all such due cautions and provisos into account, there may well be great value to letting stories and characters come alive by letting them be exactly what they are presented as, even in the Bible: namely, real stories about real people who had real beating hearts once upon a time—not unlike the real people to whom the preacher speaks each Sunday. And just this is the main point: all of these techniques aimed at enhancing sermonic vividness aim not merely at making the preacher more entertaining. Rather, these are the avenues by which the living God comes into contact with the living people listening to the sermon.

No Plastic Saints

Frederick Buechner once noted that the worst thing in the world a writer could ever do would be to set out intentionally with the specific goal of writing a story about a saint:

> Imagine setting out consciously to write a novel about a saint. How could you avoid falling flat on your face? Nothing is harder to make real than holiness. Certainly nothing is harder to make appealing and attractive. The danger, I suppose, is that you start

out with the idea that sainthood is something people achieve, that you get to be holy more or less the way you get to be an Eagle Scout.[12]

Instead, Buechner notes, sainthood is a gift of God that emerges from the genuine, often messy, lives of real people caught up in real life. "A saint is a human being with the same sorts of hang-ups and abysses as the rest of us, but if a saint touches your life, you become alive in a new way."[13] Rather than constructing a plastic person who conforms to some preconceived idea of what a saint looks like, Buechner suggests to let sainthood emerge the same way it emerged for Peter, Paul, Mary Magdalene, and all the rest in the Bible: it comes in fits and starts, dribs and drabs, and finally shines as the gift of a gracious God who saves and transforms people who, on their own, are anything but holy.

That is just the way that God reveals grace to us in our lives: God shows up in the context of the nitty-gritty reality of our Tuesday afternoons and our Friday mornings. At the end of the day, the preacher cannot really *tell* people how this goes—the preacher must *show* it. There is no better way to do that than in relaying stories that really matter to people because they resonate with those same people and with what they experience during all those many hours when they are nowhere near a church sanctuary. The need to seek out and then recognize the stories that can accomplish some of that sets the agenda for the balance of this volume, as we will probe questions related to the kinds of stories for which preachers need to be on the lookout, as well as how to nurture the habits of reading and listening that will enable preachers to locate those stories on a regular basis.

Throughout all these considerations, the goal remains constant: preachers need to present sermons that have "more reality" in them not for the sake of being interesting or relevant or cutting edge or so that the preacher can be perceived as being "with it." Rather the goal is ever and only to help the living gospel of Christ Jesus take hold in the lives of those who are seeking to follow Jesus as disciples in this world.

Chapter Two
Showing Trouble

On any given Sunday, the pains and struggles of life that people carry with them into the worship service rarely register on their faces or even through what they say as they encounter people in the church lobby before or after the service. Most people are Academy Award–worthy actors when it comes to covering up how they really feel. But the perceptive preacher knows that such hurt and trouble are there, and not just on some weeks—trouble is in the church sanctuary every Sunday. Wise preachers, then, are on the lookout for stories and vignettes that help them appreciate the depths of people's pain, stories that help them *name* pains in ways that help their sermons address this reality.

In Gary Schmidt's novel *Okay for Now*, a scene between a teacher and a teenager captures some of life's pain with gut-wrenching clarity. In the story, Coach Reed could not figure out why Doug Swieteck, one of his middle school gym students, wouldn't take his gym shirt off to play on the "skins" team during "shirts and skins" basketball games in class. Doug would always manage to finagle his way onto the "shirts" team or he'd find other clever excuses not to remove his shirt, until finally the day came when Coach Reed had had it. Coach grabbed Doug by the shirt and literally tore it off him so Doug could join the "skins" team. In an instant, the coach and every boy in the gym fell silent at what they saw. Later one of Doug's other teachers, Mr. Ferris, having heard what happened, meets alone with Doug.

"Tell me," [Mr. Ferris] said again.

So I did.

How my father came home late on the night of my twelfth birthday, and how he'd missed everything because he'd been out with Ernie Eco. . . . How he came up into my room with beer on his breath and told me we were going someplace for my birthday present and I should get dressed right now. . . . How we arrived at the mostly dark place and got out of the car and I said I wanted to go home but he looked at me with beer in his eyes and said I better get in there so I did. How I lay down on this couch and my father talked with this guy and they laughed. . . . How when it was done after a long time I looked into the mirror and saw the scroll and the flowers at each end and the words I couldn't read so the fat sweaty guy read them for me: *Mama's Baby*. And I told Mr. Ferris how they both laughed and laughed and laughed and laughed and laughed. The funniest thing in the whole stupid world: *Mama's Baby*.

How I spent days trying to wash it off, and then trying to scratch it off until it bled.

How I hadn't gone swimming since then.

How I changed for PE in the locker room stalls.

How I wished he would . . .

Mr. Ferris didn't say anything the whole time. He sat next to me and listened. And when I finished, I looked at him.

He was crying. I'm not lying. He was crying.[1]

So much of what can and often does go wrong in families, between fathers and sons, throughout the warp and woof of this fallen world can be spied in this excerpt. What in the previous chapter some authors referred to as "the grain of real life" is vividly on display in this scene—so much so that when the reader is finished reading this, Mr. Ferris is not the only one with tears in his eyes.

And all of this is in a novel written for *adolescents*.

There is much an author like Gary Schmidt can teach us, but a main item would be the fact that literature for children and adolescents does not, cannot, and must not skirt or deny the pain and the tragedies of real life. Young children have thoughts that are deep and true and very often even complex. After all, children do not live in worlds that are hermetically sealed off from reality. They come to know fear and disappointment, they experience loss and even death. Children who read novels like Katherine Paterson's *Bridge to Terabithia*, in which a key character (a young girl) dies near the end, do not, on account of having read this sad story, suddenly get jolted into a world of sadness and loss the likes of which they had never before known. No, children who read that story recognize it as belonging to the world in which they already find themselves.

But those same children know at some level that if they are going to find a way to deal with heartbreak and hope, they will do so in part through stories in which they can see themselves and through which, therefore, they can parse their feelings and come to understand perhaps a bit better how to make their way through this world. This probably explains also another piece of conventional wisdom when it comes to children's literature: any children's book that is of interest to *only* children is likely not a very good book.

C. S. Lewis and others have noted that really fine examples of children's literature are equally compelling for adults to read, precisely because the themes and the sense of reality that pervade such good children's books are universal enough to capture the imagination and the heart of adult readers, too. This explains why some years ago, parents who wanted to check out the first Harry Potter book before letting their children read it usually discovered that the child would have to wait a bit until mom and dad finished it first! Similarly, I was nearly forty years of age before I read *Bridge to Terabithia* for the first time, and yet there I was sitting on my porch with a glass of wine, reading the final page of this book meant for adolescents, and having a really good cry at how beautiful the novel's last scene was.

Children know how lovely and how dangerous, how lyric and how dreadfully sad the real world is. The novels those same children find the most compelling help them see just that world in realistic ways. This is a point that Eugene Peterson makes along the way as he comments on the David and Goliath story in his book *Leap Over a Wall: Earthy Spirituality for Everyday Christians*. David and Goliath is in some ways the classic children's story from the Bible but, of course, it is much more than that. Like most stories we hear as children, such a Bible story helps children

> develop an imagination that can recognize and explore the tensions between good and evil, love and hate, acceptance and rejection. The world is a dangerous and fearsome place: the story of Goldilocks gets us acquainted with such dark realities. The way the people closest to us treat us isn't always the truth of our lives: the story of Cinderella opens up possibilities we hadn't guessed were there. Our first impressions of what we like and dislike are often quite wrong: Dr. Seuss's *Green Eggs and Ham* prepares us for surprising reversals on what we think we like and don't like. Clearly, the stories that tell us what the world means are as essential to our growing up as the toys that show us how the world works.[2]

Denying Trouble in Worship

Stories, even (or especially) those aimed at children, reveal to us the realities of a sometimes harsh and brutal world. Children know this about the world already. But if this is so for children, it is most assuredly so for their parents and grandparents. And this straightforward yet oft-forgotten fact is the principle that underlies this chapter. The preacher must never forget that every time she stands up to deliver a sermon, she stands before people who know the hardship of life from the inside and who have already brought with them into the worship space all the cares and burdens and sorrows of their lives. These hard realities can either be engaged in preaching—thus bringing the living presence of God into contact with the things of life that vex us the most—or they can be denied in some mistaken effort to be only sunny and optimistic on Sunday mornings.

Alas, some churches and some preachers do seem to deny this fact in very overt ways, putting onto their church signs pithy (but finally impious) slogans like "We're Too Blessed to Be Depressed" or "Put on a Happy Faith!" In some worship services, chipper and bouncy "praise teams" stand before the congregation and try to suggest how everyone should feel during church by beaming forth radiant smiles as they sing songs that are often so chock-full of happiness and joy that a person on the outside looking in could surmise that there must not be an unhappy thought within a thousand square miles (or if there is, it will never have a chance to be mentioned).

Not a few preachers seem to think that what people need most when they come to worship is sound advice on child rearing or how to build successful relationships, and so they preach sermons series that are loaded with Dr. Phil–like "how to" advice. Still other preachers seem to believe that the number one need people have when it comes time for the sermon is to become better informed on the minutiae of a given Bible passage. Thus these preachers spend long stretches of their sermons explaining texts, providing information, and giving what amounts to a running commentary in verse-by-verse fashion until the preacher runs out of verses for the morning and then it's time to sing and send the people back out into the world.

Church sign slogans, overly chipper praise teams, and deeply didactic preachers all ignore a simple fact that even most young children know, much less the adults in the room: life is hard. Living as a disciple in a still-broken and frequently challenging world can be a discouraging enterprise. Try though they may (perhaps because they've been de facto told they should), most people cannot hang up and leave behind their cares and worries along with their jackets in the church lobby before entering the worship space. Sickness, death, sorrow, worry, doubts, and disappointments follow people into church, such that if the message proclaimed in the sermon is going to have any real-world traction for people, that sermon had better sketch a picture of life in which people can see the day-to-day realities of their lives and the fact that God sees and cares about these matters as well.

As one of my colleagues often notes, you cannot always see it on the outside, of course, but a great many people come to church each week metaphorically hunched over at the waist, weighed down by a host of burdens that life has laid across their shoulders in recent days. These people do not need more stuff loaded onto their shoulders. They don't need an additional load of guilt over what rotten sinners they are. They need more than just long "to do" lists from the preacher so that by following that list they can please God better in the week ahead or increase their holiness or become more moral people. They need far more than a load of new textual information piled onto them. Fred Craddock once observed that no one ever comes to church to find out whatever happened to the Jebbusites, but neither do they come needing to watch a display of the pastor's dazzling exegetical skills by witnessing the pastor point out nifty subjunctive participles in Greek or really interesting details of the Roman legal system and Pontius Pilate's place within that structure.

Acknowledging Trouble in Worship

What people need is some sense that the troubles of their lives can be brought to speech before God in a way that will make it more likely that there will be some kind of word from the Lord—spoken by the Lord's servant, the preacher—that will address them in those troubles. People long to sense that through worship and in the sermon they will experience—even if just a little bit—a lifting of those burdens from their shoulders. They listen for words that will lighten the load with gospel hope and joy, rooted in the Savior who assured his followers that his particular yoke was light, not heavy, and that lifting burdens was what he was all about.

But for there even to be a chance for that to happen, people need to have the sense that their real lives are being addressed in real ways. The preacher needs to speak in such a way and identify scenarios and questions and struggles in so vivid a manner that the people listening to the sermon will—with some regularity—have cause to say to themselves, "Hey, the preacher is talking about me! He's describing my life! She's asking the same questions that keep me up at 4:00 a.m.!" Once that happens, people listen intently not because they are narcissistic and like to hear their own situations described. Rather, precisely *because* their situations are being described, they prick up their ears to hear what word from the Lord might address them in that situation, too. To paraphrase Frederick Buechner from his book *Telling the Truth*, the "sheltering" word of hope from the gospel is of most interest to—and is welcomed the most ardently by—those who know full well that the roof had been blown off from over their heads in the first place. Actually, a great many people who gather for worship don't need to be convinced that they have lost their "roof"— they know this much already. What they need to know is that God knows about all this, and they find that out when the preacher, serving as God's spokesperson, can name the specific "roofs" people have lost and is for this reason primed to speak a sheltering word into those situations.[3]

Just this, then, is my main argument in this chapter: preachers need both to know and then overtly to acknowledge the situations of brokenness and sorrow into which they speak every Sunday. But not just in some abstract, generalized sense that yes, sometimes life can be hard. Rather the pastorally sensitive preacher and the preacher who wants to *show* trouble and not just *tell* folks about its pervasive presence in this world will want to take cues from the Bible and from ministry experience to identify and specify such trouble. As I have been asserting from the outset, what this finally accomplishes is the redemptive revelation that the living God knows about our trouble, cares for us in those hard times, and so can enter in with what will finally provide also the word of grace that people long to hear. People who come to church do not do themselves any favors by pretending that all is well because they think that is how you are supposed to feel in church. And preachers themselves do no one any favors by aiding and abetting that viewpoint by refusing to let life's more jagged edges be on display. This is surely something the Apostle Paul and Jesus knew and thus, as we will see next, the teachings of Paul and Jesus are as fine a place as any to start naming the sorrows and difficulties of our lives.

Trouble in the Bible: Epistles and Stories

The suggestion that pastors need to know about life's troubles and to name them in preaching (if not in worship generally) should not come as a surprise. The Bible itself bristles with real-life scenarios into which the word of God needs to break forth with cleansing, healing, renewing, energizing power. When in his model for preaching in *The Four Pages of the Sermon*, Paul Scott Wilson suggested that the preacher always look for what he labeled "the trouble in the text," he was not giving preachers an impossible task to fulfill.[4] Although perhaps more obvious in some texts than in others, all biblical texts emerged from a fallen and broken world, and most of those same texts, therefore, reveal difficulties or conundrums in need of divine address and redress. Very few of Paul's New Testament epistles, for instance, can be read without it being obvious what difficulties the members of his congregations were facing. Some of those difficulties may have been self-inflicted, and others may have been inflicted on them by the world or by the trying circumstances of everyday living.

What is clear throughout his epistles, however, is that the Apostle Paul was keenly aware of the situation facing his readers. The Thessalonians were upset that members had died before Jesus came back and fretted what happened to those souls. The Galatians had reverted to all the worry and one-upmanship that attends those who become convinced that achieving salvation is in no small part up to each one of us to accomplish. The Corinthians could not stop fighting over a whole laundry list of divisive topics, even as Philemon had to be instructed on what to do—and even how to feel—over against a runaway servant. Paul had just the one gospel to preach at the end of the day, but he brought that living gospel into contact with the real-life situations of his congregations in ways he clearly hoped would gain traction in their midst by virtue of his having connected with their actual situations in that particular moment.

The need to have such real-life traction persists today. Some years ago when I was a pastor, a man who was not a member of my congregation but who received written copies of my sermon each week wrote to me while I was in the midst of a sermon series on Genesis. There is no honest way to preach on many of those narratives without taking note of the brokenness that attended the relationships between Jacob and Esau, Rebecca and old Isaac, Jacob and Laban, Joseph and his brothers. The man who had been reading these sermons had himself experienced significant pain with a couple of his own children, and so wrote to me to say how curious it was to him in middle age to notice something that few if any preachers had ever pointed out to him earlier in his life: namely, there are very few families in the Bible that could not fall under the heading of "dysfunctional." He found this fact to be both remarkable and oddly comforting in that the same Bible that did not try to airbrush the image of these fractious families also talked about those same families precisely because somehow, some way, God's grace was operative in the midst of all that unhappiness. A family did not have to have it "all together" for God to be at work. God was active in these biblical families not despite their brokenness, but as often as not precisely *on account of* that dysfunction. Such a thought gave this man hope.

Parabolic Trouble

Displaying a realistic sense for life's troubles was a thought not lost on Jesus either. Across the last two millennia, a host of ways have been concocted by which to parse, categorize, and interpret the parables of Jesus, as well as his teachings generally. But weaving in and through all those theories and constructs there remains a core of realism to the teaching and preaching of Jesus that ties in well with what we are talking about in this book, and more specifically in this chapter. Jesus told parables whose bottom lines were sometimes mostly about grace, sometimes more about judgment, and oftentimes about describing the kingdom of God and how grace and judgment emerge in and through the in-breaking of that kingdom. According to one traditional framing, Jesus's parables were "earthly stories with heavenly meanings." But that is far too simple, as that definition removes the bottom line meaning of parables too far from real life, from this earth.

In truth Jesus's stories were very earthly both in terms of narrative content *and* in terms of where the grace of the kingdom needed to shine forth. Jesus described real situations not as a way to elevate people above all such daily realities but as a way to reframe that reality and infuse it with the presence of God after all.

But it is Jesus's identifying of the troubles of our lives that is as revealing as anything. When Jesus told stories, they almost always included elements of life's frustrations and hurts. Various parables acknowledged that widows exist in this world and that their lives are hard and are sometimes made more difficult by unjust judges and others who just don't care. In his parables Jesus named for his listeners situations of injustice, of loss, of carelessness, and of disappointment. The parables showed what today we'd call dysfunctional families as well as vignettes of social injustice and inequality. The parables acknowledged that we live in a world of crime and a world in which criminals also not infrequently get away with their crimes, leaving the victims to suffer. Parables talked about people of enormous mercy and people who seemed to have no mercy in them at all. Parables depicted really smart people, really savvy people, really careless people, really industrious people, and really lazy people.

Today we have often sufficiently rarefied the parables of Jesus to the point that they scarcely need to touch the reality of our world in order to deliver the bottom line of teaching that we think is the only point to these stories to begin with. What we forget in so doing, however, is that whatever other effects—immediate and long-term—that Jesus's parables had on those who first listened to them, surely one of the things that happened in the minds and hearts of those listeners was their saying to themselves, "Yup, I know somebody like that," or, "Hmmm, seems to me I feel that way myself many times."

What we forget, in short, is that Jesus's parables had traction in real life precisely because they were so good at *describing* real life in the first place. Jesus's original listeners would not have surmised that these little tales were all about other people from faraway times and places. On the contrary, they would have known that it was they themselves and their lives and their circumstances that were being described. That's why they listened: to see if the living God could really show up inside those troubles with a presence and a grace that would help. Jesus was so good at this that it is rather natural to wonder how he did it so well. Could it be that he paid really good attention to life?

Of course, whenever you deal with Jesus, it's always a little dodgy to know how to bring his divine nature into interaction with his human nature. This is especially true when it comes to Jesus's engaging in the eminently human activity of learning. If in the carpentry shop Joseph showed Jesus how to use a planer, did Jesus really have to pay attention or did he—as divine—know all that stuff about every single tool in the shop already; in his mind's eye, could he see clear ahead to the era of electric saws and belt sanders? If Jesus went to school and listened to a teacher explain arithmetic, did Jesus only pretend to learn that 2 + 2 = 4 or was he doing high-level calculus and quantum physics in his head already anyway? There's no definitive way to answer such wonderings, but since it seems doubtful that Jesus would ever have deceived teachers or parents and since the Gospels indicate he seemed to learn as he went through life, perhaps we can at least safely assume that as a true human being, Jesus possessed the ability truly to learn, too. No doubt, among the things he learned along the way were the situations of what in this chapter we are calling the trouble of life.

The Power of Observation

Perhaps one of the reasons Jesus was able to infuse his parables with such an air of reality that so well described human struggle, sorrow, disappointment, joy, and all the rest is because for all those years before he ever opened his mouth to speak a parable, Jesus had been a keen observer of life. He'd been to both weddings and funerals. He'd witnessed both generosity and stinginess, both great justice and great injustice, both happy families and fractured families, both rich people and desperately poor people. He had seen what makes people burst out in laughter and what makes people recoil in sorrow; both what can elevate the human spirit and what can shrivel such spirits through withering scorn and sharp criticism. Jesus had observed and witnessed it all in the fullness of his being fully human and this, then, enabled him to teach and preach and tell parables that went on to reveal what a difference kingdom grace can make in all these daily realities of grief and trouble. Jesus could well have donned the t-shirt that my wife once wore home from her time at the Iowa Writers Workshop years ago: "Just Researching My Novel . . ." Good writers and good preachers are good observers at all times. Or as Alyce McKenzie puts it in the title of her blog, preachers need a "Knack for Noticing."

Please note that such a knack reveals a vital principle and practice for preaching: preachers pay careful attention to life's angularities because—as was noted in chapter 1—if it is true that the devil is in the details, then the need for God's mercy and grace is usually spied in the details, too. This is something Jesus knew and preachers do well to know it, too, as they observe the grain of real life all around them and into whose snarled details they preach every week.

But this is a principle surprisingly easy to forget or ignore. In my own tradition there was a time when those who taught preaching essentially told future pastors that the main thing about making a sermon was to get the exegesis right. Once you had your passage exegeted up and down, forward and backward, the sermon was about 95 percent complete: just tack on an introduction and maybe a conclusion and you were finished. (And as noted above, if you were Karl Barth—though he often did not follow his own advice—then you'd avoid even introductions and conclusions, as they merely impede the preacher's ability to do what is the sole task of preaching: viz., just repeating exactly what the text says.) But today most preachers know better and are taught better, too.

In his own preaching, presumably the divine side of Jesus "knew" in some sense everything that needed saying. Think of that as the exegetical side of preaching today: preachers have the divinely inspired word of God in front of them, and that word already contains everything the sermon needs in terms of bottom-line teaching content, as well as our deepest hope and our joy in the gospel. But even Jesus himself was not ready to preach until he had done his homework on the human side of things also, through his learning about the struggles and the joy of real life in the world. Think of this as the human side of preaching today also, as the *content* of God's word simply must be brought to bear on the real-life *context* of this present day. If in the end we want God's grace to burst upon people's consciousness as a reality of everyday life, then the trouble that cries out for that intervening goodness of God needs to be named clearly and well to provide the opportunity to see that grace in action.

Naming Trouble through Story

There is a whole lot of pastoral experience, wisdom, and observation that goes into that contextual component of preaching, but this is also precisely the part of preaching that needs to do what this volume is telling preachers they must do: find those stories that matter. A great deal of what follows will be to suggest how to find such stories in the arts and such, but, of course, even those stories are useful for preaching only insofar as the preacher knows that they touch on the reality of the congregation's experience and circumstances. Often if a preacher finds a story from some other source—a novel, a film, a newspaper article, a documentary—that the preacher knows will be of value in a sermon somewhere, the reason is because the preacher knows his or her congregation sufficiently well to know that this story names something already present among the people who listen to sermons every week.

In *Imagining the Kingdom*, James K. A. Smith notes at one point that we should not discount the stories gleaned from novels or films merely on account of their being fictional:

> I have been influenced by James Woods's account of the novel in *How Fiction Works*. Discussing issues of "realism," he notes: "Brigid Lowe argues that the question of fiction's referentiality—does fiction make true statements about the world?—is the wrong one, because fiction does not ask us to *believe* things (in a philosophical sense) but to *imagine* them (in an artistic sense)."[5]

In other words, when you see a fine film or read an excellent novel, the question of whether or not something really "happened" in actual history is less important than seeing a plausible narrative of something that could have happened precisely because as a matter of fact such things *do* happen every day. If a novelist presents a scenario—a scene inside the novel, much less the narrative arc of the entire story—about which most readers would say, "Oh for heaven's sake, everyone knows that *that* could never happen!"—then the novelist has failed at his or her vocation.

Years ago I heard the novelist Tom Wolfe say that the world has become such a bizarre place, in which so many unlikely stories actually take place every day, that one could almost pity novelists whose imaginations cannot keep up with real-life events. Yesterday's "that could never happen" scenario is tomorrow's "breaking news" on CNN! But the point here is that although relating fictional stories in preaching may be a step removed from telling a "true" story of trouble based on real experience, that does not lessen the value or the impact of such stories. If people can see the concrete difficulties of their lives inside fictional narratives, then the only truth that matters is the listener's own truth as he or she sees his or her own troubles of life reflected in the narrative vignette that has been shared in the sermon. (And anyway, few if any in the history of the church have ever complained that Jesus's parables are not worth considering, seeing as characters like the persistent widow in Luke 18 or the gracious king in Matthew 18 never actually existed in real life. In the life of the church, we are long accustomed to seeing deep truths emerge through "fictional" stories.)

Even so, it is the case that some of the most poignant stories a preacher will ever find will be the ones that emerge from real life, from pastoral encounters, from simply walking with people through life's highs and lows. Not all those stories can be shared overtly from the pulpit, and the preacher must never tell a story that he or she has no right to share or reveal something that is not his or hers to reveal. Above all, preachers must never betray a confidence—the preacher cannot tell specific stories about specific people without the permission of the people involved. In many sensitive cases, the preacher would not be granted such permission even if it were sought. However, real-life hurts can be more safely described when the stories that convey such trouble are fictional, emerging from a novel or a film in a way that betrays no trust and risks no breach of confidentiality but that still names hurts that are common to all.

What every preacher knows and must consistently remember is that the word of God preached from the pulpit must intersect with the troubles that people bring with them into the worship space every week. And there may be no better way for the Holy Spirit to do that through a sermon than by having the preacher tell stories that reveal the very situations, questions, struggles, and hurts into which the word of God needs to speak.

Eliciting Real Life

Sociologist Roman Williams engages in a fairly new sociological research method called "visual ethnography," which is a way to conduct studies of people and people groups using primarily visual methods. A key practice in this area of inquiry is called "photo elicitation" and the way it works is pretty simple: the subjects of a given study (say, international students studying in the United States, such as Williams himself researched as part of his graduate work at Boston University) are given disposable cameras and asked to take pictures of their ordinary, everyday lives. Later the pictures become the focal point for conversations with these subjects as they narratively fill in the background stories behind each image. Typically the resulting photos fall into the categories of "Inventories" (pictures of someone's collection of books, photos of a bedroom, shots of someone's office cubicle and its contents), "Events and Activities" (pictures of birthday cakes, shots of anniversary parties, photos taken while out on a bike ride or while taking a hike), and "Institutions and Processes" (pictures of work settings, photos of people hunched over desks or working on a machine or riding a tractor in a field of wheat).[6]

What such pictures do, of course, is reveal the very "grain of real life" that was discussed in chapter 1 when pondering why showing is always more effective in storytelling and preaching than telling. After all, once the people who took the photos have a chance also to tell the stories behind the images, even more of the contents of people's lives begin to emerge. Williams and others have used this method to do studies of people's spiritual narratives as they seek to spy where religion and religious practices pop up in ordinary situations.

But when I heard of this, immediately it was clear how much pastoral potential this contained for leaders in the church. Imagine a pastor providing cameras to various members of his or her congregation as a way to gain a virtual window into the lives of the very people to whom he or she preaches every Sunday morning. It is not difficult to see how quickly a pastor would gain a fuller sense of what people do every day, and what situations of trouble they regularly face, in ways that would almost certainly have an impact on the specificity of examples and stories the preacher could bring into sermons when trying to describe real-life situations of need, want, or hardship, as we are thinking of these things in this chapter.

Of course, it is likely that even if a pastor literally did this, there would be much about people's lives that would never be photographed. Some things would remain properly private. But through the use of the pastor's imagination, it would not take long before a pastor could summon to mind those other images that would never actually be taken by a camera but that surely exist every day. One could see in the mind's eye the image of a man or a woman sitting in a living room with work-weary eyes at the end of a long day on the job. What's the story behind those tired eyes? Can one spy the questions of how they can keep up this pace, how long they can keep working too hard for too little money? Can a pastor imagine the photo that could be snapped while a mother is on the phone with her wayward and rude daughter—could one imagine the pain and the disappointment on the mother's face and then further fill in the narrative background that would be behind those doleful facial expressions?

Whether the preacher literally elicited stories by having congregants snap pictures in a kind of congregational visual ethnography, or whether the preacher used the concept of photos taken from everyday life to extend his or her imagination into the lives of those who listen to sermons, the point is that sermons always enter into lives that have just that specificity, just that level of visual and emotional detail. Thoughtful pastors will always be on the lookout to gather up the stories and narratives that can capture what people experience and then will use those stories in their sermons so as to evoke the real world in which people are called to live out their faith every week.

In what follows, this chapter will suggest several categories of what we could label "trouble" in people's lives and then suggest further where stories could be found that will illustrate such real-life situations and for that very reason help listeners see themselves inside the picture the sermon is sketching. Such categories of trouble emerge from the Bible generally, as noted above, and from the framing of many of Jesus's own parables. As just noted, when thinking about the pictures that could be taken of the congregation in the average week, these kinds of trouble represent pastoral common sense: any reasonably experienced preacher will already know that these are the circumstances into which he or she preaches each Sunday—it is just a matter of not forgetting this in the busyness of "getting up" a sermon every week. The real-world traction of the sermon will always be enhanced by finding and including stories that matter.

Although such categories could easily be multiplied—and although each of the following could be accompanied by also multiple subheadings—in what follows this chapter will focus on the following broad areas of human Trouble:

The Pain and Dysfunction of Families

The Sorrow of Broken Dreams and Dashed Hopes

Human Character and Sin

The Struggles of Loneliness

This is not an exhaustive list, of course, but in my experience as a pastor, these particular aspects of trouble in life seem more often than not to be among the key hurts that burden the hearts of those who come to worship each week.

The Pain and Dysfunction of Families

According to the oft-quoted first line of Leo Tolstoy's novel *Anna Karenina*, all happy families pretty much resemble one another, while all unhappy families are quite different from one another. It's a curious observation for Tolstoy to make, and it's an open question how much research he ever did to back up such a claim. But once a person has been in ministry long enough, it becomes sadly clear that there really are a staggering number of ways through which families can go bad. True, there are some broad patterns that can be traced involving rebellious children or combative spouses or the pain that adultery and other forms of unfaithfulness bring into people's homes. But for all the feelings and actions that are the same across this unhappy landscape of familial dysfunction, there is also that variety of circumstances to which Tolstoy referred. C. S. Lewis noted in his book *The Four Loves* that if it is true within marriage and family that we have the opportunity for the sweetest love and fellowship—sweeter, in fact, than may be possible anywhere else in life—the obverse is regrettably also true: those same family settings are the location for some of the deepest hurt human beings are capable of inflicting on one another.

In the last quarter century there has been a lot of talk—emanating mostly from church circles—about "family values" and the need to help build strong marriages and strong family units. This is a noble goal and an apt one for the church and its leaders to pursue and promote. Of course, as noted above, the Bible itself may not always be the best resource for providing vignettes of happy and intact families. Whether it's Jacob resorting to military-like tactics in preparing once again to encounter his estranged brother Esau after many years of Jacob's living on the lam or David's wrenching cries of "O Absalom, Absalom, would that I had died instead of you" echoing along the corridors of scripture, the Bible does not hide the fact that even the families of people inside God's covenant were not always happy places.

The New Testament itself shows Jesus pulling people away from their families so as to form a new "family" of disciples, and apparently this pattern persisted, as historians of the first and second centuries in the Roman Empire have noted that the Christian church did have a way of breaking up families. If push ever comes to shove in terms of loyalty to Christ over against loyalty to a family of origin—and in many places in this world this is still the case—scripture makes it clear that faith and not family must be paramount; that, in fact, brothers and sisters in Christ become one's new family.

The "Perfect Family" Myth

Yet it is typically the case that we all would just as soon not let any of that show on the outside of our families. As the BBC sitcom character Hyacinth Bucket knows (and be sure to pronounce that last name as "bouquet"), nothing is quite so important to people in modern societies as *Keeping Up Appearances*. We want to "keep up with the Joneses" not only in terms of having a car or a boat or a swimming pool as nice as our neighbors, but most especially in terms of conveying that our lives are as happy, settled, and tranquil as their lives appear to be. We all tend to believe that other families—including other families within our church communities—have it all together in ways we struggle to achieve.

In an early scene in the movie *Jerry Maguire*, a single mother is sitting on an airplane with her young son. They are just close enough to the first-class cabin as to be able to overhear the animated talk of a passenger who is describing his travels, his exquisite relationship with his significant other whom he will soon marry, and other sundry details that all sound glowing and positive. At one point the single mother sighs audibly at what she's hearing, prompting her little boy to ask, "What's the problem, Mommy?" "First class is the problem," she replies. "It used to be just a better meal, now it's a better life."

Of course, in that movie viewers soon find out that the man doing all that bragging about himself is the character of Jerry Maguire, whose life is anything but stable and ordered and good. But we all tend to do what the single mother did: we look across the aisle or across the church sanctuary, we see other families leading lives that surely look very different from how we view whatever is going on in our own lives at the moment, and we assume all is well. The so-called golden families are in every congregation. These are people who seem financially stable, if not well off, whose marriages seem strong and exciting, whose children are all like the kids in Lake Wobegon: above average. The kids are successful in sports, are handsome and beautiful, and are most assuredly going places. Soon we find ourselves wishing we were like them, that our kids were like their kids, our marriage like their marriage.

Even pastors can be lured into looking at only the surface features of people's lives, and so may assume that all is well in the lives of most families to whom they preach every Sunday. Sometimes, of course, things happen that shatter this image of familial bliss, and the pastor is now and then among the first to find out: an adulterous affair breaks out into the open and a seemingly strong marriage ends in tatters or one of the golden children of the family is arrested for cocaine possession, and this once apparently intact family now divides along various responses to this event (even as these parents now have to visit their child through plate glass at the local prison). Soon much that had looked stable and solid and secure looks shaky and on the verge of collapse.

Thankfully, however, such dramatic breaches of family unity remain relatively rare in any given congregation. But what preachers should never forget is that even absent something public that causes everyone to revise their assessment of a given family's relative happiness in life, just below the surface of many families there are heartache and wounds aplenty. In fact, if I recall some of the most terrible things that I as a pastor learned about certain families across the years, the reality is that to this day very few of the other people familiar with that same family have any clue as to the depths of hurt that are present there. We refer to familial pain and past hurts as "skeletons in the closet" for a reason—they do tend to stay "closeted" away and well out of most people's sight.

Naming the Pain

The thoughtful preacher, then, simply must look for ways both to understand the contours of this pain and to address it pastorally in sermons. Since it can be difficult—if not impossible—to share from the pulpit the actual stories of dysfunction or familial despair of which a pastor may now and then become aware through pastoral counseling and other encounters—and since some pastors are blessed not to know this kind of pain firsthand based on actual experience—preachers can often be helped by skilled novelists, whose stories are able to describe in vivid details the pains and hurts and disappointments that often come to characterize the lives of even apparently "golden families." Such fictional novels may provide preachers with stories that can be safely shared from the pulpit. But fictional though these stories are, to many of the people listening to the sermon, the descriptions may well sound eerily familiar. They will readily be able to identify their real lives and the situations they face all the time. What follows are a few examples of such revealing stories that I gleaned from some novels I read over the years. I present them here not only for their own value but as inspiration for all preachers constantly to be on the lookout—in reading, watching movies, and observing life in the congregation—for similar vignettes that uncover the very familial trouble into which the word of God must be spoken.

Some novels succeed painfully well in telling searing stories of pain and brokenness. Among a few contemporary such books are *American Pastoral* by Philip Roth, *The Corrections* by Jonathan Franzen, and *We Were the Mulvaneys* by Joyce Carol Oates.

First, consider how the trajectory of the lives of many people in this world—and how the process by which even rock-solid families can dissolve into chaos—is captured by Roth in his novel just by the titles of the book's three main sections: "Paradise Remembered," "The Fall," "Paradise Lost." (One wonders how many real-life people in our congregations might be able to name the segments of their own lives in such biblical terms.) Along the way in *American Pastoral*, we learn the story of Swede Levov, a dashing high school athlete whose life seems charmed, until one day his daughter commits an unspeakable act of violence after which, bit by bit, life falls apart for this family.

As the story opens, the narrator tells us that once upon a time, no one could think of anything better than being this person. "The Swede. During the war years, when I grew up, when I was still a grade school boy, this was a magical name in our Newark neighborhood, even to adults just a generation removed from the city's old Prince Street ghetto. . . . The name was magical."[7] By the time the novel ends, the narrator has this to say: "They'll never recover. Everything is against them, everyone and everything that does not like their life. All the voices from without, condemning and rejecting their life! And what is wrong with their life? What on earth is less reprehensible than the life of the Levovs?"[8] Obviously what takes place between that opening and that closing is a story of tragedy that can be difficult to read. But what preachers gain by immersing themselves in such a story is a keen pastoral sense of what it feels like from the inside to watch a once-promising family fade away. Even if most of the families who gather for worship on Sundays do not represent the extreme dissolution of the Levov family in Roth's novel, it certainly may well be the case that hidden near the hearts of many families are the pains, disappointments, tensions, and sheer bewilderment depicted in a story such as this one.

Pastors who make themselves aware of such disorientation can name this in their sermons and then seek to find the word of grace that needs to enter into such situations of hurt. Learning about such pain in some detail becomes a homiletical strategy to bring this particular, albeit very unhappy, note of realism into sermons. Of course, novelists have done their job once they depict the despair. A novel such as Roth's can end on the unhappy note sounded in the quote above. But preachers cannot end merely with portraits of sorrow. Rather, this becomes the necessary bridge to the gospel, and it is a bridge that needs to be built again and again, of course. Taking that next step to introduce the good news of God's grace will be taken up in the next chapter. But people need to know that this grace *can* enter even into the jagged contours of their own families, and there may be no better way to help them believe that than to hear the preacher do a good job in describing the details of their familial hurt.

A second example of familial pain comes from Joyce Carol Oates. Because she is adept at weaving in many quotes from the Bible as well as many pieces of traditional piety, Oates's work in *We Were the Mulvaneys* may strike even more chords for the pastors who read this tale of the golden family that also falls apart. Situated in a rural community called Mt. Ephraim, New York, the Mulvaney family—father, mother, three sons, and one daughter—were the envy of all who knew them. In the opening chapter "Storybook House," the narrator (who is Judd Mulvaney, the youngest of the four children) says, "We were the Mulvaneys, remember us? From summer 1955 to spring 1980 when my mom and dad were forced to sell the property, there were Mulvaneys at High Point Farm, on the High Point Road. . . . For a long time you envied us, then you pitied us. For a long time you admired us, then you thought *Good—that's what they deserve.*"⁹

What accounts for the change of status over the years for the Mulvaneys? It was everything that happened—everything that was done and said—in the years after Valentine's Day 1976, when the daughter, Marianne, was sexually assaulted by a local boy from her high school on the night of the prom and after the dance. What is shocking about Oates's insight into life is how relatively thin the wall may be between everything running smoothly in a family's collective life and everything falling apart. How could God let anything happen to Marianne, after all?

> [Marianne] was so pretty. So radiant. No other word: *radiant.* The kitchen bulletin board, Corrine's [the mother's] province, was fes-

tooned with snapshots of Marianne: receiving a red ribbon for her juicy plum-sized strawberries a few years ago at the state fair in Albany, and last year, two blue ribbons—again for strawberries, and for a sewing project; being inducted as an officer in the Chautauqua Christian Youth Conference; at the National 4-H Conference in Chicago where she'd won an award in 1972. Most of the snapshots of Marianne were of her cheerleading, in her Mt. Ephraim cheerleader's jumper, maroon wool with a white cotton long-sleeved blouse. The previous night Michael [the father] had taken a half dozen Polaroids of Marianne in her new [prom] dress, which she'd sewed herself from a Butterick pattern.[10]

How many houses don't have bulletin boards with pictures of children like the one described here? But in how many households don't events transpire as to unravel—even retrospectively—all that can seem golden and good about life? As the reader watches the effects of Marianne's rape tear into the life of one Mulvaney family member after the next—and as the sheer amount of secrets that they all begin to keep from one another mounts—one gets a firm sense of how sin and evil can engulf even the best of us, leaving people dazed and confused as to how it could possibly be that the lives of good Christian folks could end up the way they sometimes do. This is a kind of family-based trouble about which we pastors need to know and about which we need to talk in our sermons. These are precisely the situations in which people need to see the living God entering into their hurt—naming the hurt specifically, then, becomes the bridge for bringing in the gospel of God's living presence in Christ.

When we preachers are able to engage real hardships, probably more people than we could guess will listen to the sermon from the perspective of those who have had front row seats to just these feelings, just these events, just these disorienting situations of loss and disappointment. Put simply: the ability to articulate in some detail this kind of disorientation is a vital tool that needs to be in every preacher's tool kit. This is not something designed just to make a sermon interesting or lively—this is a homiletical practice that gives the sermon the pastoral traction that will root the message deeply into people's hearts.

A third kind of pain on the home front reminds us that the hurts and the events that shake things up don't always have to rise to the level of complete dissolution. Good storytellers like Anne Tyler can reveal the more everyday slights and wounds that trouble us. Consider this excerpt from a sermon I once preached on the healing of the ten lepers from Luke 17, in which I used Tyler's character of Delia Grinstead:

> In her book *Ladder of Years*, novelist Anne Tyler introduces us to Delia Grinstead. Delia is a lovely, loveable, and utterly giving wife and mother who regularly does her level best to keep her household running smoothly. But as her children grow up, they become "great, galumphing, unmannerly, and supercilious creatures" who ignore Delia and who flinch from her hugs. What's more, they expect that their favorite foods will always be in the pantry or the fridge, but they never thank Delia for purchasing these sundries (though they will complain loudly should she forget one day). Meanwhile, Delia's husband is so wrapped up in his medical practice that he, too, brushes past Delia day in and day out, regularly failing to notice the spic-n-span house, the clean laundry, the warm food set before his distracted face each evening.
>
> After years of this neglect, Delia begins to feel like "a tiny gnat, whirring around her family's edges." Their ongoing lack of gratitude has killed something in Delia—not all at once, mind you, but day by day Delia dies a little, wilting like a flower that receives too little moisture. She doesn't even realize how dead she has become until one day she meets someone who is kind, who thanks Delia for a little something. This stranger's kind gratitude is like a few precious drops of water applied to her soul—a few little thankful droplets that reveal just how dry, cracked, and barren the landscape of her soul had become.
>
> Finally the day comes when Delia just walks away from her family. She's taking a stroll on a beach and just keeps on going. Once her family realizes she is missing, they have a curiously difficult time describing Delia to the police. They just can't seem to recall the color of her eyes, her height or weight, what she was

wearing when they last saw her. Of course, they'd never really seen her to begin with. They had been blinded by ingratitude.[11]

Unexpressed thanks is an insidious way to hurt someone. A sin of omission if ever there were one, a lack of thanks-giving is a passive form of verbal abuse. We all know how we can wound people through what we actively spew out of our mouths. But silence can have a heft all its own—failing to thank people is an emptiness with substance, a gratitude vacuum that suffocates. As Lewis Smedes reminds us, life is out of joint when we fail to give thanks. The insensate way by which some people receive and receive and receive yet without ever saying, "Thank you" is a baffling phenomenon—baffling, it seems, even to God.

The sermon then went on to connect the ingratitude of the nine lepers to this portrait of what ingratitude felt like to—and what ingratitude ultimately did to—someone like Delia. By being aware of this particular narrative portrait, not only was I able to provide a vignette of ingratitude in action as a way to connect to the story in Luke 17, but I was also able to connect this to what goes on in a lot of households all the time, so as to suggest that the grace of God that saves us in Christ can and should have a lot to do with how we treat each other in our families. We often picture the family dinner table as the place where love is expressed and where family unity is thickened, but as Tyler reminds us—and as many of those who listened to this sermon already knew—those same tables can be places where all the rough edges of our lives can be seen and where the sometimes very *un*loving ways by which we often treat one another in our families are put on grim display. But for that very reason these are the situations that good preaching aims to talk about and reveal, so that the word of the Lord that comes through the sermon may have something to say in those very same situations.

The ability to name this type of pain is one of the finest acts of pastoral care the preacher can provide inside the sermon. But familial pain is not the only type of hurt people bring with them to church. They bring with them also broken dreams.

The Sorrow of Broken Dreams and Dashed Hopes

Probably the single most well-known song from the musical *Les Miserables* is "I Dreamed a Dream." It always brought the house down when *Les Miserables* was a Broadway stage production, and the awards Anne Hathaway went on to win for the 2012 film version could be attributed in no small measure to how powerfully and mournfully she belted out that same song. But the song brought down not just the house but something closer to the whole world when an unknown, somewhat doughty, forty-eight-year-old woman named Susan Boyle sang it on the television show *Britain's Got Talent*. When Ms. Boyle looked into the camera and sang the song's tagline, "Now life has killed the dream I dreamed," the sheer heartbreak of the sentiment caused watchers on YouTube to puddle up with tears for weeks and weeks, as the clip was downloaded tens of millions of times.

Thankfully, and also with a nice bit of irony, for Ms. Boyle that performance actually became the gateway for her to *realize* her life-long dream of becoming a famous singer. If only this were closer to the rule than the exception it actually is. The reason why "I Dreamed a Dream" has long been so popular—and the reason most people are moved by the song—probably ties in with the fact that most people can identify with the disappointment of unrealized dreams and aspirations. Our lives are frequently fraught with scenarios of the "what if?" variety as we wonder if we made the right choices about our education, our career, the opportunities that came but that also then went.

The Pain of Regret

Although pastors get to know plenty of senior members of the congregation who are blissfully blessed to look back on seventy, eighty, or ninety years of life in which things turned our more or less the way they had once dreamed they might, there are many others who look back with bitterness, disappointment, and heartache. They could never have children of their own and adoption never worked out either, and so they passed into their later years alone. Or they did adopt a child but never had any grandchildren (and wouldn't that have been nice?). Or they look back on all they did with their working years and wonder if maybe there had not been something else, something better, something more productive they could have done instead. Such regret is unhappily very common.

In the opening scene of the Alexander Payne film *About Schmidt*, viewers meet Warren Schmidt on the day of his retirement, after having spent his entire career working as an actuary for the Woodmen of the World insurance company in Omaha, Nebraska. Warren and his wife, Helen, go to a local steakhouse to attend his retirement dinner on a rainy Omaha evening, and in the after-dinner speeches it's clear that try though they may, most people found it hard to say a whole lot as to the meaning of Warren's work across the many decades. Sensing this, Warren excuses himself from the banquet for a bit, ostensibly to go to the restroom. But actually he wanders over to the restaurant's bar and orders a stiff drink to numb the chagrin brought on by his own retirement nontribute.

A week or two into his retirement, as Warren finds nothing to do, he visits the young man with an MBA degree who replaced Warren to see if he had any questions that Warren could help him answer. But no, this young man needs nothing Warren could give ("Heck, a business degree ought to be worth something!"), and so after a brief encounter Warren leaves the building only to see, next to the dumpster, boxes and boxes filled with his old files. His entire lifetime of work would soon be scooped up and dumped into a landfill. Reflecting on this, Warren laments that it's clear he's made very little difference in this world and when soon he dies—and as an actuary Warren can even calculate with some degree of accuracy when that will happen—it will be only a matter of time before no one on earth will ever know he even existed.

Although this movie ends with a lilting moment of grace, the basic plot is hardly cheery. Yet many people who come to church each

week bear in their hearts pangs of disappointment and the emptiness of unfulfilled dreams. This kind of nostalgic regret may be more
prominent among some older members of the congregation, but a
sense of longing, a restless feeling of incompleteness, attends people
of all ages, including those approaching middle age and even younger
people who are perhaps dealing with the limits they've already encountered or who live with the nagging fear that they will grow up
to be just like their disillusioned, unfulfilled parents or grandparents.

Trapped by Despair

In the realm of literature few writers in recent times have captured the frustration of life's limits and the disillusionment of unfulfilled dreams better than Russell Banks, particularly in some of
his earliest novels. In *Continental Drift* and *Affliction*, Banks adroitly
displays what it feels like to feel trapped inside one's own life with
few if any chances to escape life's limits so as to arrive at some other,
better place. The epigraph from Simone Weil from which Banks got
the title of his novel *Affliction* points to this dimension of our world:
"The great enigma of human life is not suffering but affliction." Precisely because Banks can put readers in touch with the afflictions
of life, his work can be difficult to read, as it contains rough language and depicts situations fraught with sin and brokenness. But his
novels succeed in depicting, with searing poignancy, the despair felt
by many. Consider this description of where the character of Wade
Whitehouse lives in *Affliction*:

> The trailer at the very end, a light-blue two-bedroom unit with
> rust gathering at the seams, was parked on what might have been
> promoted in the beginning as the most desirable lot in the park.
> It was next to a short crescent of beach and, on the other side, a
> sharply narrowing point of land, so there was no room for adja-
> cent trailers. This was the home and lot that Wade Whitehouse
> had purchased from his boss, Gordon LaRiviere. . . . Wade was
> broke, but LaRiviere offered to hold a twenty-year mortgage with
> no down payment, and he gave Wade first choice of all twelve

trailers in the park. It was July, and Wade thought he liked to fish; and the little beach next to the light-blue Bide-a-Wile looked like something he would enjoy, especially in the warm summer evenings after work. As it turned out, however, he never got around to buying a fishing rod. And he had not used the beach once in two years, partly because he was so busy in the summer months. . . . Then came his first winter at the trailer park, and with that it became obvious that the place at the end of the row of trailers out on the point was in fact the worst location in the park. It was the place most exposed to the cold winds that swept off Parker Mountain and, picking up speed as they crossed the lake, banged like hammers against the tin sides of the unprotected trailer before swooping on toward the White Mountains beyond.[12]

As the story continues, the place where Wade must live becomes emblematic of all that he feels is wrong with his afflicted existence. The very best he could afford was, in the end, paltry and pathetic, and what little promise the place seemed to offer initially proved in the end—like everything else in his life—to be hollow and just out of reach for one reason or another.

Even more searing is Banks's description of the main character of Robert Dubois in *Continental Drift*. Notice how swiftly Banks sums up the way life looks to a lot of people:

Dubois thinks, a man reaches thirty, and he works at a trade for eight years for the same company, even goes to oil burner school nights for a year, and he stays honest, he doesn't sneak copper tubing or tools into his car at night, doesn't put in for time he didn't work, he doesn't drink on the job—*a man does his work*, does it for eight long years, and for that he gets to take home to his wife and two kids a weekly paycheck for one hundred thirty-seven dollars and forty-four cents. Dirt money. Chump change. Money that's gone before it's got. No money at all. . . . He is a frugal man. He owns a run-down seventy-five-year-old duplex in a working-class neighborhood on the north end of Butterick Street, lives with his family in the front half and rents out the back to four young people he calls hippies. He owns a boat, a thirteen-foot Boston whaler he built from a kit, with a sixteen-horsepower Mercury outboard motor; the boat he keeps shrouded in clear plastic from November until the ice in the lakes breaks up, the motor he keeps in the basement. He owns a battered green 1974 Chevrolet station wagon with a tricky transmission. He owes the Catamount Savings and Loan Company—for the house, boat, and car—a little over $22,000. He pays cash for everything else. He votes Democrat, as his father did, goes occasionally to mass with his wife and children and believes in God the way he believes in politicians—he knows he exists but doesn't depend on him for anything. He loves his wife and children. He has a girlfriend. He hates his life.[13]

The title of the chapter that tells us all this and more is titled, very simply, "Pissed." Bob senses his life is over, that he can keep on keeping on for another three or four decades with precious little prospect of anything changing in any significant way. He works hard and yet comes home to furniture that is just sufficiently tattered and frayed as to remind him of his every limitation. It reminds one of the scene in the movie *It's a Wonderful Life*, in which George Bailey goes up the staircase of his drafty old house only to have the ball on the banister come off in his hand as goes by. A flash of frustrated fury crosses George's face and he clearly wants to hurl that wooden ball as far as he can. But instead he angrily slams it back into place. Sometimes it's the little things in our houses or in our lives or at our jobs that seem to stand as a symbol for everything we wish were different.

Why should preachers read scenes like these last two from Russell Banks? Part of the reason ties in with the "Show, Don't Tell" we discussed earlier: these scenes are vivid, loaded with detail and the grain of everyday life. They remind preachers of the specific features to life that often bring people down due to their inability to make things better: drafty trailers, battered old cars for which a person is still in debt, hard-earned paychecks that have no chance of making ends meet, much less getting a person ahead a little bit in life.

But a larger reason to be exposed to such searing portraits of despair is to connect with a way of life that some preachers may know firsthand but that many others will have no personal access to. Many people are blessed enough to grow up in homes where if something breaks, it gets fixed; if some piece of furniture wears out (even a little), it gets replaced. Family vacations got financed with the extra money dad or mom brought home and there was never any real question or anxiety about coming up short. There is much for which to be grateful in that kind of life but it hardly describes everyone who listens to sermons on Sundays. Many people feel trapped in a deadening cycle of one unfulfilling day and week and month after the next.

Consider another such vignette from a different source: the Bill Murray movie comedy *Groundhog Day*. The up-and-coming Pittsburgh weatherman Phil Connors finds himself trapped in what he regards as the hick town of Punxsutawney, Pennsylvania. Having gone there with his two-person film crew to cover the annual Groundhog Day weather prediction by the groundhog known as Punxsutawney Phil, Connors discovers that every morning when he wakes up, it is once again February 2, but only he is aware that he is reliving the same day over and over again (for up to ten years' worth of Groundhog Days, according to the film's director). On one of his thousands of February 2 days, Connors is at a bowling alley one night along with two working-class stiffs from the town. At one point Connors reveals his plight by saying to these hapless fellows, "What would you do if you were stuck in one place and every day was the exactly the same and nothing you did mattered?" After one of the men knocks back a numbing shot of whiskey, the other replies, "That about sums it up for me."

It sums it up for lots of people. The feeling of being dead, of being stuck, of working hard for too little pay characterizes the lives of many people to whom we preachers speak in every sermon. Of course, in a volume such as this one we can just glimpse what writers like Russell Banks sketch at much greater length in their novels, but the experience of immersing oneself in an extended story such as is told about Bob Dubois forms one's sensibilities and sensitivities in ways that properly shape the way we address life's disappointments and hardships in sermons. These are not easy stories to read, but they are necessary stories of which to be aware.

When Dreams Decay

Again, however, my argument here is that the sensitive pastor will want to know these hard truths so as to be able to bring them to speech—and so bring also this aspect of reality—into the preaching moment. Across any given pastor's preaching life—and when considering any number of biblical texts on which a sermon could be based—there are occasions when articulating life's disappointments will arise, if only the preacher has sufficient awareness of these issues as to be able to name them. One such occasion in my own preaching when I tapped into such disillusionment with life was in a sermon based on a passage that itself could come from a Russell Banks novel, Ecclesiastes 12:1-5:

> Remember your Creator
>   in the days of your youth,
> before the days of trouble come
>   and the years approach when you will say,
>   "I find no pleasure in them"—
> before the sun and the light
>   and the moon and the stars grow dark,
>   and the clouds return after the rain;
> when the keepers of the house tremble,
>   and the strong men stoop,
> when the grinders cease because they are few,
>   and those looking through the windows grow dim;
> when the doors to the street are closed
>   and the sound of grinding fades;
> when people rise up at the sound of birds,
>   but all their songs grow faint;
> when people are afraid of heights
>   and of dangers in the streets;
> when the almond tree blossoms
>   and the grasshopper drags itself along

and desire no longer is stirred.
Then people go to their eternal home
and mourners go about the streets.

In the opening of the sermon on this passage, I used a real-life vignette that resonates with the sad disappointment of lost and decaying dreams that we have been pondering in this section. Notice how this description of a town in decline is like an almost exact echo of those words from Ecclesiastes 12:

A little over a week ago, the *New York Times* published a front-page story on a little hamlet in upper New York State called Newton Falls. Newton Falls sprang to life around 1894 when a large paper mill was built in that part of the northern Adirondacks. In the century since then this mill has provided work for hundreds and hundreds of Newton Falls residents and was the employer of 125 people as recently as four months ago. Except now the mill is closing and Newton Falls, according to the article, is teetering on the verge of communal death. The hamlet still has about a hundred residents, but not much more than that. In addition to the mill, the Newton Falls Hotel with its small pub is about the only thing left, aside from the small-ish, working-class style houses that make up the local neighborhoods.

Once upon a time Newton Falls was a busy, close-knit small town with close to a thousand residents. In the century of its history Newton Falls, like most such towns, has been home to many people who dreamed dreams, baptized their children, sent sons off to war, and mourned their dead. Life happened there, in other words—real life with all its wrinkles, beauties, special moments, sorrows, joys, and just overall variety of experiences.

But now it will soon be a memory, and not much of a memory at that. Even local history books that chronicle upper New York State include just a slim paragraph or two about Newton Falls. The archive of the Saint Lawrence County Historical Society has only a handful of old brochures from the mill and a few undated, early-twentieth century photos of some unidentified men toiling around large rolls of paper at the mill. But that's it. The A&P

burned down some years ago and was never rebuilt. The barber-shop closed, followed by the bowling alley. Now with the mill going down the tubes as well, the tiny school will almost certainly fold, as in all likelihood will the twenty-bed local hospital which, as it is, averages only two patients per day.

Abandoned shops, empty factories, boarded-up windows, undated photos of unidentified folks whom no one even remembers anymore: it's Ecclesiastes 12 in a contemporary nutshell. The planet keeps spinning, time keeps passing at its relentless pace, and even the best life has to offer fades into memory, and then into an oblivion where even memory winks out. Life, the Teacher might say, is like some faded and yellowed photograph on the wall at your great-grandma's house. Someone snapped that picture because the people in it were precious and loved. Someone framed and hung that photo because it was an image and a memory worth savoring, worth glancing at again and again. But now it's been in the sunlight too long. The photo-sensitive chemicals have decayed such that now you cannot even make out who was in the picture, and there is no one left alive who could tell you.

Have you ever been in one of those antique shops that sells not just old furniture but old *everything*, and in which just about every nook of that shop has not just furniture, lamps, and paintings but knick-knacks and bric-a-brac of every kind? Every once in a while when browsing through such antique shops you run across a shoebox full of old, black-and-white photos. And suddenly you come face to face with all these strangers staring out at you: wedding photos of people who as often as not hardly *look* like this was the happiest day of their lives; little children gussied up for the photographer and perfectly posed on a little footstool; portraits of older men and women who look like there is much on their minds, much they would like to tell you, but in the silence of that moment frozen in time you cannot hear their voices, cannot read their thoughts.

Have you ever run across such a cache of photos? If so, has it ever depressed you utterly? One day will my picture or your picture end up in such a place, being gawked at by strangers who don't know our names, will never know who we were or what made us laugh and cry? Is this what life comes down to: ghost towns and forgotten lives?

Granted, this is not cheery stuff for your average Sunday morning! But the Bible passage itself was unstinting in its assessment of life. Like young people who read well-crafted children's books that do not deny life's darker realities, so also many people who hear sermons like this one will discover *not* that they are learning for the first time that life has disappointing and distressing limits, but that they can see themselves inside that picture already. Thoughtful preachers will evoke scenarios such as Newton Falls not in order to bring into the preaching moment a darkness that would not otherwise be present in a worship service. No, the purpose is to *name and acknowledge* what altogether too many people listening to the sermon know painfully well already. This honest acknowledgment, then, becomes also the occasion for bringing in the word of grace and hope. The sermon that began with Newton Falls ended this way:

> Newton Falls is a town that looks to be winding down. Some of us know firsthand how that feels. Yet Newton Falls did have its day in the sun, did have a time when good lives well lived happened there. Most of us have had such times, too. When such times come to an end, memory can transmute into nostalgia, a word that means "the pain of the past." But if we remembered our Creator in the days of our youth, if we led a life that had a living connection to God in all those times *before* retirement came and before the spring went out of our step, then maybe memory itself becomes infused with grace.

> As Frederick Buechner once wrote, looking back on our lives, we can all be a little amazed and plenty grateful that we made it this far at all. There were so many times when it could have all ended for us, so many times when we could have given up on God or God on us, so many times when those closest to us had every good reason to tell us to take a hike, but they didn't. That we made it this far at all is itself a kind of grace, and a gift too.

Remembering your Creator will not change your status as a limited person in a life that as often as not zips right past us. But maybe, just maybe, remembering God infuses the fleetingness of this life with intimations of that eternity that, as the Teacher said in Ecclesiastes 3, God has set into our hearts. To be alive in the mind of God is to be alive indeed. How can we know that we have found a nook in God's living memory? We know it, we are engulfed by it, every time we hold nuggets of bread and cups of wine as we hear, "Do this in *remembrance* of me." We remember Jesus, and he remembers us. We remember Jesus, and he reminds us that we have never been alone. We remember our Creator who has promised that he will remember us. Always. Even to the very end of this otherwise meaningless age. We remember. God remembers. And so together we are alive to one another. Always. Alive.

The dreams and aspirations of our lives do not always pan out. Whether we are like Warren Schmidt looking back on a career we deem insignificant or working-class folks whose tireless labor seems to yield only more tiredness; whether we live in homes that now and then seem dilapidated or feel utterly stuck in a situation a million miles from where we thought we'd end up, the brutal fact is that many of us live with at least low levels of disappointment and sometimes very high levels of dissatisfaction.

As noted earlier in this book, we are fundamentally "storied animals" who understand and make sense of life in narrative terms. If the gospel is going to reach into our lives, we need those lives described in sermons through images and realistic stories that reverberate with everyday life. For many people, if they hear stories coming through in the sermon that accurately describe the flat and disappointing landscapes of life, such a sermon will capture the hearts of many listeners in that they will sense their own reality being named. It is when someone listening to a sermon can say (like the man in the *Groundhog Day* bowling alley), "That about sums it up for me," that the Holy Spirit can then wing also the grace and hope of the gospel into those very situations.

Human Character and Sin

Not all of life's trouble comes on us unbidden. Sometimes the source of our pain is the amazing complexities of human sin, and among the key places where preachers can learn about the curious, crafty, and finally also perilous ways sin snarls human hearts is through works of biography. Skilled biographers like the writer Robert Caro expose the sins and temptations with which all people struggle by highlighting such sin in the lives of famous people. As Neal Plantinga has pointed out, it might seem an odd thing to assert, but the fact is that preachers need to know a lot about sin if they wish to know just how and where the gospel needs to encounter the people who are in need of grace's forgiveness. Preachers need also to know that talk about sin from the pulpit cannot always be restricted to sex, drugs, and alcohol, which in at least some of the preaching I have heard seem to be the go-to sins to which preachers sometimes restrict their focus. An honest examination of human life such as can emerge from biographies reveals that sin is far more subtle, insidious, and multifaceted.

For instance, President Lyndon Baines Johnson was a man of significant, even outsized, abilities on a variety of levels. Throughout his life he used his keen intellect and preternatural political instincts for both significant good and devious self-promotion. It is generally acknowledged that Johnson and his team stole the 1948 Senate election in Texas, first by a smear campaign of a genuinely good man (Johnson's opponent was the extremely popular former Texas governor, Coke Stevenson), and then second through outright chicanery at the polls. After the votes were tallied, Johnson received credit for hundreds of votes that were most certainly not cast for him. After the election, and when it was too late to do much about it, an election official discovered one curiosity on the ledger from precinct 13: someone had taken a pencil and neatly added a half-circle to a seven, thus changing it to a nine. With that jot of pencil, LBJ's vote total in precinct 13 jumped from 765 votes to 965.

Matters were odder still in another precinct, where this official noted that the last two hundred people who voted *all* voted for Johnson. In a close election that fact would be odd enough. But the election official then looked a little more closely at the precinct record sheet on which registered voters signed in. Those last two hundred names, it was clear to see, were all in the same handwriting and in alphabetical order from A to Z, and then starting over at A again. What was going on was clear enough, but for the sake of thoroughness the official did a random sampling and went out into the precinct to interview a few of these folks. Quite a few indicated they had not voted for either Johnson or Stevenson, seeing as they stayed home and didn't vote at all. Still others on that list of two hundred final voters did not vote that day, either, but they had an excuse: they were long dead and buried in the local cemetery.

Johnson won his seat to the United States Senate in 1948 by a margin of eighty-seven votes over Governor Stevenson.[14]

Once Johnson got to the Senate via this corrupted election, his career proceeded forward, until he finally landed in the Oval Office fifteen years later, after the assassination of John F. Kennedy. Along the way, Johnson used his parliamentary skills first to block every effort at civil rights legislation that came before the Senate and then, in the late 1950s when Johnson realized his anti–civil rights stance was hurting his chances ever to become president, Johnson reversed course and rammed through the first civil rights legislation in nearly a century. As biographer Robert Caro has noted repeatedly throughout his multivolume series *The Years of Lyndon Johnson*, Johnson was a man of significant ambition and deep compassion, including compassion for the down-and-out in society. When Johnson was able to get his ambition and his compassion running together on the same track, great good ensued, including the Voting Rights and Civil Rights Acts passed under his presidency in the mid-1960s. As Neal Plantinga has often put it, Johnson is a classic example of how God can hit straight shots with crooked sticks.

Unhappily for Johnson, however, ultimately his ambition and the devious, secretive tendencies that were lodged deep in his heart would prove to be his undoing once he doubled down on Vietnam and refused to acknowledge errors or tell the full truth to the American people (and maybe he managed to keep the truth from even his own self). At the end of Caro's fourth volume, *The Passage of Power*, Caro notes that somehow from the time of Kennedy's assassination until the middle of 1964, Johnson managed to corral and control his demons and his most despicable tendencies. In so doing, Johnson seemed like an agent of divine providence, helping a grieving nation find its feet again and so move forward despite the loss of such a dynamic young president.

Johnson's transition to the presidency under dreadful circumstances is a remarkable story of steadiness and compassion. But as Caro writes at the end of that fourth volume,

> The story of the presidency of Lyndon Johnson [is] different in tone from the story of the transition in part because the elements of his personality absent during the transition were shortly to reappear. . . . If he had held in check those forces within him, had conquered himself, for a while, he wasn't going to be able to do it for very long. But he had done it long enough.[15]

But it did not last. Only a few years later, America's initially modest involvement in Vietnam would swell to the point of 58,000 men dead, 300,000 wounded, and untold numbers (though some say it could be two million) of dead Vietnamese citizens. Johnson would eventually refuse to run again for president in 1968, returning to his ranch in Texas to live out his days, with the haunting chant, "Hey, hey, LBJ, how many kids did you kill today?" providing the grim soundtrack for his final four years of life.

Reading the story of someone like Lyndon Johnson provides the preacher with many vignettes and anecdotes of what corruption and self-deception look like in action. More than just examples, however, delving deeply into the character of someone like Johnson provides wisdom and insight into the nature of humanity, in ways that can help sermons describe reality with sufficient insight and specificity that the people listening to the sermon will recognize their own struggles with sin and temptation, and so make them hungry for the answering word of grace.

The Contradictions of Character

Preachers never address a congregation that is either singularly saintly or singularly sinful. Instead sermons enter into the prolix and turgid territory of the human heart, where at any given moment most people sense urgings and tendencies toward great nobility and terrible selfishness. If we marvel that someone like Lyndon Johnson could be both egotistical and compassionate at the same time, perhaps that is because we have not honestly assessed our own states of being during the course of any given average day. In the New Testament, James notes the curious fact that the same mouth that can offer praise to God can also be a font of cursing and angry words. James could have gone on to note that sometimes that same mouth can pivot from the one to the other at the proverbial drop of a hat. As a preacher, I wish this were not so, but I confess that there were Sundays when in the morning people thanked me for speaking God's truth in the sermon, yet on the evening of that same Sunday I sometimes snapped angrily at my wife or kids.

Such crosscurrents and the overall complexity of human character is on display all through scripture, too, although in its typical style, scripture is spare in describing this, leaving it to preachers and all readers of the Bible to bring to bear on the text larger insights from life. By delving deeply into the biography of a Lyndon Johnson or a Golda Meir, preachers can begin to understand the layered and sometimes contradictory nature of human character.

This kind of insight might help preachers supply some of the necessary background to understanding someone like Jacob in the book of Genesis. Despite the cleaned-up versions of this story that many people learned in their Sunday school days, the fact is that Jacob was a riven character, beset by ambition and possessed of a keen intellect that made it pretty easy for him to get what he wanted in life by duping, tricking, and often outright lying to the people closest to him. Whether it was a simple matter of luring his somewhat dim-witted brother into a bad bargain or a more carefully crafted plot by which to exploit his dear father's near-blindness, Jacob knew how to get ahead in life by living off his own wits. This would go on for years—including the many years when Jacob sparred with his equally devious Uncle Laban—until finally God quite literally wrestled Jacob to the ground to show him what's what and who's who in the grand scheme of things.

All in all, it's a fascinating story, but isn't it equally fascinating to ponder how Jacob lived with himself during all those years of wheeling and dealing? What went through his head? Did he ever feel guilty? How could he be both tender and loving toward some and bare-knuckled and hard-nosed toward others? And why did God stick with him all that while? In fact, since we know from the outset of the entire Jacob cycle of stories that Jacob is the favored one of God to begin with, we can wonder why God insists on hitting straight shots with crooked sticks. Why not start with a straight-stick kind of person in the first place?

But we can ask similar questions about Moses, Deborah, Miriam, Saul, David, Sarah, Peter, and Paul. The characters we meet in scripture are not so very different from the people who listen to sermons week in and week out. Many biblical characters are like the rest of us: they are not two-dimensional and are almost never straightforwardly (or consistently) good, nor ever and only wicked (even wicked King Ahab managed some genuine repentance after Elijah confronted him for his sins against the innocent man Naboth in 1 Kgs 21).

Again, scripture does not try to provide a thorough biography of any of these people and is not given to long ponderings as to the crosscurrents of their personalities. But just that provides the opening for preachers to help the readers of the Bible—and those who listen to sermons based on that Bible—to bring other insights about human character to bear so as to deepen insight and provide that connection point between scripture's stories and all of our stories yet today. The writer Marilynne Robinson asserts,

> If Western history has proved one thing, it is that the narratives of the Bible are essentially inexhaustible. The Bible is terse, the Gospels are brief, and the result is that every moment and detail merits pondering and can always appear in a richer light. . . . In comparison with other ancient literature, the realism of the Bible is utterly remarkable—so we can bring our own feelings to bear in the reading of it. In fact, we cannot do otherwise, if we know the old, old story well enough to give it a life in our thoughts.[16]

Varieties of Sin and Its Fallout

The principal strategy at work here is for preachers to be always learning about the angularities of real life in order to be able to describe this accurately and with deep insight. When it comes to sin's influence in life, few of the people listening to a sermon will begin to pay more attention to the message of the sermon just by hearing vague, generalized descriptions of sin. It is only when a significant degree of specificity is mentioned that listeners begin not only to see themselves inside the picture the preacher is sketching but to understand that the accuracy of that portrayal is precisely why any given person needs to tune in to the message.

If you tell me, "Sometimes we all make mistakes," I will lightly nod my head and shrug my shoulders as a way to say, "Yeah, I suppose that's true." But if you tell me, "Sometimes we'll throw almost anybody under the bus if that's what it takes to keep ourselves from being seen in a bad light," now I am connecting that to a time or two in the last few months when I engaged in precisely that kind of cruel, self-protective behavior. Now I am remembering how I made it look like the project I messed up was really my colleague Jeff's fault, even though I knew better. Yes, we all make mistakes but I made *that* one. By mentioning it so specifically, you now have my attention.

Preachers need to get people's attention. This is true not just in terms of sin but in terms of everything we have been discussing and will yet discuss in this chapter. People need to know that the sermon is talking about *their* hurting families, *their* disappointments and broken dreams, *their* sinful tendencies and practices, and (as we will see in this chapter's final section) *their* loneliness and isolation.

One way preachers accomplish this is by reading widely enough as to discover kinds of sinful behavior—and the pain it brings to others—that extend beyond both the preacher's own experience and perhaps beyond what some people think of when they think generally about sin in life.

For instance, people who grew up in loving families, in which parents took a healthy interest in the well-being of their children, could perhaps not imagine what others have experienced when parents are callous or so focused on themselves as to give their own children only a passing glance now and again. But any number of people who listen to sermons know that kind of pain and so perhaps will see themselves reflected in sermons now and then if a preacher can tell a story like this one from William Manchester's biography of Winston Churchill—a story that I once used as an opening illustration for a sermon delivered at a youth-led service in my congregation:

> When Churchill was still very young—seven or eight years old— he was packed off to boarding school. Not surprisingly, he quickly became enormously homesick. So he would write pathetic letters home to his mother, begging her to come visit him, pleading with her to arrange it so he could come home for the weekend sometime. But Winston's mother had never really had much time for her son—she was far too wrapped up in a busy social life. So when she received her son's earnest letters begging for some love and attention, she usually just tossed them aside. Indeed, Churchill biographer William Manchester once made a sad discovery. While looking through some boxes of Churchill's old letters and diaries, he ran across one of those letters in which young Winston begged his mommy to come visit him at school. But not only had his

mother ignored this plea, she had even used the backside of the letter as scratch paper on which she scribbled out a guest list for a party she was planning to throw the next month.[17]

More than just an arresting, compelling, and finally also sorrow-ful story, such a story may well uncover for a preacher significant layers of pain from people's real-life experiences—a deep personal wound in desperate need both of acknowledgment in sermons now and then and in need of the healing touch of God's grace in Christ through the gospel.

Stories from the news or from books of history and biography are also a rich trove for illustrating various specific sins, including those core attitudinal sins usually referred to as the seven deadly sins. Although each of those sins can be described and defined using what in the previous chapter we called the language of "Tell," listeners understand the essence of these sinful dispositions best when the preacher can "Show" them in action.

In a sermon on Exodus 5, I once described Pharaoh as a good ex-ample of a proud person—someone so elevated in his own eyes that it never occurred to him that there might be Someone above him. "Who is Yahweh that I should listen to him?" was his sneering reply to Moses when Moses confronted Pharaoh with God's desire to free his people from Egyptian slavery. To introduce that sermon I reached for one of the many vignettes of pride that William Manchester pro-vided in his biography of the great General Douglas MacArthur in the book *American Caesar*:

> General Douglas MacArthur was easily one of the most vain and proud men of the twentieth century. Even people who were on a first-name basis with world leaders knew better than to address MacArthur as anything other than "General." Even MacArthur's *wife* called him General! He had no diminutive and would abide none. Had someone ever called him "Mac" or "Doug" to his face, the response would have been arctic. MacArthur wanted and needed to be revered. So he installed a fifteen-foot high mirror right behind his desk to increase his stature in the eyes of people

who entered his office. He insisted on being photographed as often as possible with pictures of Lincoln in the background so as to invite interesting comparisons. He also developed the habit of referring to himself in the third person ("MacArthur will be leaving for Fort Meyer now").[18]

Most people who listen to a sermon in which a story like this might be shared may not know anyone with the kind of obvious, outsized pride of a Douglas MacArthur, and neither should a preacher talk about pride as though it were visible *only* when something this striking is on display. However, we may also come to know the contours of pride in our own lives—smaller and subtler though its expressions may be—when we can see those contours writ large in the lives of others.

Similar observations can be made about pride's first cousin, the sin of envy—most people struggle with envy at least a little, so seeing it on grand display may help those who listen to sermons detect it in their own patterns of behavior. It seems as though at any given moment the news contains at least one sordid story about someone seeking quite literally to cut a rival down to size. In the mid-1990s such a story came from the world of Olympic figure skating. The lovely and graceful Nancy Kerrigan was quite simply a bit better on the ice than another very talented skater named Tonya Harding. To Tonya's mind, she was forever dwelling in Nancy's shadow, and Tonya did not much enjoy the publicity chill she got in that shadow. So with key competitions coming up and the Olympics in view, too, Tonya sought to elevate herself by bringing her rival down a few pegs: she hired a thug to whack Nancy in the kneecap. If Tonya could not outshine Nancy, she'd sideline Nancy as a shortcut to glory. (Nancy did sustain a severe injury to her knee, but once the story broke out into the open as to how that attack came about, it was Tonya who was forever sidelined, eventually opting to try to eke out a living in the world of roller derby.)

When a story like this is in the news, it illustrates envy in a startling way but also becomes the story that provides the homiletical opportunity to help listeners recognize concretely and with startling clarity where those very same tendencies lurk in all of our hearts. The same is true of a story like this one that I used in a sermon on envy from Numbers 12, when even Aaron and Miriam oddly enough seem to envy their brother Moses.

The following illustrative tale cuts a little closer to a church setting—and a lot closer to how even preachers sometimes think:

> Martin Luther King Jr. was one of the twentieth century's finest preachers and orators. Already while he was in seminary King's sermons shined for their depth of insight and rhetorical power. But while it's easy for *us* to admire Dr. King's skill, matters were not so simple for his seminary classmates. To them King was not a rising homiletical star to admire but rather a peer who, annoyingly enough, garnered all the praise of the faculty even as he received far more requests to preach in area churches than did any of his classmates. All in all, Martin was a prime target for envy.
>
> A most egregious example of such envy happened after one of King's earliest seminary sermons, a stunning message titled "The Three Dimensions of a Complete Life." King preached this sermon one Sunday at a church in Montgomery, Alabama. The very next week one of King's seminary classmates, Walter McCall, was scheduled to preach in this same church. So McCall swung into the pulpit the next week with his own sermon titled, "The *Four* Dimensions of a Complete Life"! Not surprisingly McCall's clunky, envy-driven attempt to one-up and outdo King resulted in a poor sermon that made King's sermon look even better by comparison![19]

Probably no phrase of the Reformation scholar Martin Luther has been quoted more often than his observation that even as Christians we exist *simul iustus et peccator*, righteous and sinful, justified and yet still struggling with sin at the same time. No honest person has ever demurred from Luther's insight. As someone once observed, there is no necessary contradiction between being in a worship service praising God and yet having the wolves of sin howling in one's soul.

In the final scene in the Sinclair Lewis novel *Elmer Gantry*, the shifty, philandering evangelist is kneeling in church, bewailing the sins of which he had been accused and sobbing forth his repentance. Yet as the preacher kneels in penitence on the platform in the front of the church sanctuary, he glances up long enough to take note of the lovely ankles attached to the young woman who had recently joined the church choir. Rev. Gantry noted to himself that *this* was a young woman he'd have to get to know better . . . but the thought was so quickly registered in his mind that it did not even interrupt the flow of the prayer he was even then uttering aloud for all to hear!

As noted earlier in this chapter, odd though it sounds, preachers must know a lot about the very sin we all despise but to which the gospel is God's ultimate answer. Sermons that seek pastoral traction in people's hearts and lives need to tell stories and provide vignettes that target and name the angularities of our often riven characters. Those who listen to sermons cannot look for and celebrate the manifold ways by which God's grace in Christ can penetrate their real lives if they cannot sense in sermons an honest acknowledgement of daily struggles with sin.

Lifting up the flat rocks of our lives and seeing what is crawling and squirming underneath should never count as one of the preacher's chief joys—that should be reserved for what we will talk about in the next chapter, in the proclamation of grace—but unless the preacher is alive to the news stories and history books and biographies and pastoral encounters that uncover the complications of human character, it becomes much less likely that listeners will see themselves sufficiently in the picture as to become hungry for the true grace that alone can, bit by bit, restore us to the true image of God in which we were created and toward which we are being daily recreated by the Spirit of Christ, as we mature more and more into Christ, our Head.

There is, however, one last kind of trouble we will consider in this chapter: loneliness.

The Struggles of Loneliness

In Advent one year I preached a sermon from Isaiah 53 titled "Wrong Side of the Tracks." Ultimately the sermon reminded listeners that for the sake of our salvation, God the Son became incarnate by coming not to the wealthy or elite of his day but to an ordinary family with limited means. The sermon began this way:

A while ago in a series of articles looking at poverty in America, *The New York Times* published an article that centered on a thirteen-year-old girl from Dixon, Illinois, named Wendy Williams. Based on the story it appears that Wendy is a bright, sweet girl from a stable, two-parent family. She loves her pet cat, Katie, and has an aptitude for art and math. Wendy has a lot going for her, yet she spends most of her days struggling to hold onto her self-esteem. Because, you see, Wendy lives on the wrong side of the tracks, and the other kids don't let her forget it.

Wendy lives in a mobile home in a tin-plain trailer park with the unlikely name of "Chateau Estates." Her father works hard as a welder but earns only nine dollars an hour. Her mother spends a few hours a week as a cook for a Head Start program, but also earns very little. So in a school full of kids who look like walking billboards for names like Nike and Tommy Hilfiger, Wendy must walk around in rummage-sale slacks and belts bought at the Farm & Fleet, attire that her classmates do not hesitate to call "tacky." While her fellow students talk about their new thousand-dollar computer toys and look forward to their family's next trip to the Caribbean, Wendy must face a reality in which her family cannot afford the forty-five-dollar fee now charged to play school sports. Even on those occasions when Wendy finds cause to smile, she hides her smile behind her hands so that no one will notice the overbite that her parents cannot afford to get fixed and that once earned her the nickname "Rabbit."

A girl like Wendy just doesn't fit in a school full of children who have grown up as the targets of savvy marketing campaigns by J. Crew and Walt Disney. The expectation of prestige and wealth is so common now that the teachers at Wendy's school report that all of the kids they meet these days say when they grow up, they want to be doctors, lawyers, or professional athletes—anything that will earn them gobs of money and prestige. A vocational teacher in the local high school complains that he can't get anyone to sign up for courses that teach skills like the tool-and-die trade. Even though such jobs can earn seventy thousand dollars a year, many kids believe that salary would be too low.

So Wendy Williams spends her time trying to hold onto enough self-esteem to stick with her studies so she can avoid the fate of her three older sisters, all of whom finally gave up on high school, dropping out to have babies. It's not easy, though: at the end of each school day, Wendy's bus stop is first, and so all of her more wealthy classmates get to watch Wendy as she shuffles toward her trailer, face down, eyes fixed on her generic tennis shoes.

In a world where money counts, where image is everything, and where the incessant hype of the celebrity-driven media invades every segment of life, folks like Wendy don't fit. Such common, low-income, nonglitzy people don't register on the media's radar scope. Even an article as poignant as the *New York Times* piece probably didn't make any impact on the words and attitudes of those who routinely make Wendy so uncomfortable. Feel sorry for her if you wish, but Wendy and her family won't serve as anyone's role model.

Even her parents hope that Wendy will herself one day achieve something better. For how painful it is to see your child be humiliated. Wendy's mother, Veronica, sadly told the *Times* reporter of her inner anguish at seeing her daughter come home from school more often than not with her head bent low because once again someone had reminded Wendy that her attire and lifestyle don't make the grade.

Of course, what we routinely forget, even as Christians, is that according to the Bible, the salvation of the cosmos also emerged from the wrong side of the tracks. As Isaiah predicted and as the gospels confirm, when the Son of God came down to this world, he lacked everything that would catch people's eyes. Born in a barn to low-income parents, Jesus was raised in the ancient world's equivalent of a run-down trailer park in the little podunk back-water of Nazareth. He wasn't particularly handsome and seemed so meek as to qualify as shy. No one thought he was a bad person, just an unremarkable one, that's all.

Thanks to the incredibly good writing of the *New York Times* reporter who presented Wendy's story, a lot of what was discussed in the previous chapter is on display here, including key details that both helped listeners picture Wendy and her home in their imaginations and that contained more than a little of "the grain of real life" that teachers of creative writing often talk about. More than just a vivid vignette, however, Wendy's story named a feeling of isolation and loneliness that a great many people experience. In this particular sermon, this also became the point of contact to remind everyone that when it came to knowing how it felt to be Wendy Williams, no one was going to have greater empathy and compassion than the Savior born in Bethlehem's stall. When it comes to being born on the wrong side of the tracks, Jesus understands.

That is going to be a piece of good news to many people in the church as well, because loneliness and a sense of social isolation are more rampant than preachers may sometimes believe. Of course, those who are economically much better off than Wendy's family are not for that reason immune to loneliness in their own lives. Loneliness can and does come to people from all walks of life. Listen to people long enough and it soon becomes clear that often even those members of a congregation who seem reasonably well connected are finally rather lonely. How easy it is to look at a woman whose husband died, perhaps even quite a few years earlier, and conclude, "She has really done very well with it all." But what most people cannot see is the ache in her heart, the tears on her pillow that come when she wakes up at 3:00 a.m. and still absentmindedly reaches for the body that has long been absent from that other side of the bed.

We often call our congregations a "fellowship" of believers, and never is that community on better display than on Sundays when everyone gathers for worship. But many people know what it is like to feel alone in a crowd, even at church, and how quickly that fellowship seems to dissolve once the couples and the families of the congregation all scatter back to their individual homes.

If we could peer into some people's homes, we might well see loneliness more often than we'd ever guess. It reminds me of the Alfred Hitchcock film, *Rear Window*, in which Jimmy Stewart plays L. B. "Jeff" Jeffries, a professional photographer who has become laid up with a broken leg. With nothing to do for weeks on end, he takes to peering across the courtyard of his New York apartment complex to observe the lives of his neighbors, often using his telephoto lens for a better view. (Think of this as a kind of vicarious version of the visual ethnographic practice of "photo elicitation" mentioned earlier in this chapter.) One woman in particular frequently arrests Jeff's attention: a woman he takes to calling "Miss Lonelyhearts." It is obvious she is indeed a lonely person, sometimes waiting for dates who never arrive to pick her up and other times actually staging a dinner as though she had a companion across the table from her. One evening while Jeff watches more of this sad spectacle, he witnesses Miss Lonelyhearts going to her bedroom, flinging herself onto the bed, and weeping bitter tears. As he turns away from this scene, the look on Jeff's face tells viewers that he wished he had not seen that. It was heart-crushingly sad. But how often might we all witness such scenes if only we could, like in *Rear Window*, see what is otherwise hidden from the world by the walls and window shades of our homes?

Of all the features to real life that sermons seek to narrate and reveal and name, the loneliness of life in the modern world counts as among the sadder situations that are known to many people who sit in churches every week. Thoughtful preachers will scour the news and watch intelligent films and read insightful novels to find stories that probe the depths of isolation and what this does to people's spirits day by day. When preachers can name this in their sermons, then the gospel once again has a whole new set of opportunities to enter into people's hearts.

Some years ago in a sermon from 1 Peter 2, I was struck by Peter's turn of phrase when he tells his readers that "once you were no people." Peter's epistle may be a couple thousand years old, but it struck me that Peter was naming something we know about all too well in the modern world, and so that sermon opened this way:

Whatever you may think about the musical group the Beatles, it is generally acknowledged that few bands have ever paid as much attention to the lonely, invisible people of society as did the Beatles. Two of their songs carry a particular poignance in this regard. One haunting tune is titled "Nowhere Man." The song talks about a lonely and isolated man to whom no one pays any attention: the man, his work, his hopes and dreams do not register with a single other soul in the world. But in the end the song asks, "Isn't he a bit like you and me?"

Perhaps the most poignant such song is "Eleanor Rigby," which paints a sad vignette of lonely people who live on the isolated margins of the wider world. Eleanor Rigby, we are told, is the caretaker of a country church. Eleanor is the one who picks up the rice after weddings have come and gone. The church's pastor is Father McKenzie, a man who, it is said, writes sermons for worship services that no one attends. At the end of the song lonely Father McKenzie buries lonely Eleanor Rigby after the poor soul dies and is buried "along with her name." The mournful chorus of the song wonders both where such lonely folks come from and where in the whole wide world they might ever find a sense of belonging or community. But as Christian people should know better than anyone, the truth is that we are surrounded by all these lonely people all the time.

Years ago when I was a seminarian, I used to make calls on neighborhood people to bring them food from my congregation's food pantry. It often amazed me that sometimes, even when people would invite me to sit down and chat for a bit, they never turned the TV off. I found it annoying and vaguely rude. But later I realized: that TV and the sounds it makes was this person's only companion day in and day out. They'd no more turn the TV off than you'd stick your best friend out in the garage.

83

Recently a sad story was published in the *New York Times* about how the "Meals on Wheels" people in the city recently adopted a cost-savings plan. Instead of bringing a hot meal to elderly people *every* day, they could save time and money by bringing them a week's worth of ready-to-be-heated meals on Monday only. It made good economic sense, but the people who received the meals were bitterly disappointed. You see, for many of these New Yorkers, the "Meals on Wheels" person was the only other human being they ever saw most days. But now it would be just once a week. In a city of eight million, they are alone.

The article featured a heartbreaking photo. We all know that famous painting of the bearded grandfather praying with bowed head and folded hands at a table on which there is a bowl of soup, a loaf of bread, and a big Bible with the man's glasses on top. That is a heartwarming, classic painting that, inadvertently, the *Times* mirrored. Because in their picture they showed an elderly lady, head bowed and hands folded, praying over her "Meals on Wheels" dinner even as she sat in front of, not a Bible, but a small black-and-white TV that was still on. That is her life.

"Once you were no-people," the Apostle Peter wrote. Once you were no-people. Once you were nobody, a nowhere man or a nowhere woman, a marginalized and isolated cipher ignored by the world and off floating on society's fringes. No-people. That, Peter tells his readers, is who they had once been. Nobodies belonging to no one in particular and going nowhere special in life. No-people. Can you hear the aching sadness in that?

If you can, then the lyric and lilting nature of this passage can hit home. If you can sense the longing behind what Peter is saying, then you will also sense afresh why at the center of our Christian experience is this sacrament called Holy Communion. Because in this passage Peter makes clear that if you want to talk about the mass of this world's lonely, rejected people, you would have to place Jesus in their number.

In this particular sermon excerpt I brought out several related portraits or stories of loneliness from popular music, pastoral experience, and yet another revealing expose of real life from a newspaper article (all of which is why the answer to the question, "Where can I find good stories for my sermons?" is "Just about anywhere and everywhere you can think to look!"). Each of these vignettes seeks to accomplish what has been the stated aim of this book from the outset; namely, to get "more reality" into the sermon so that our day-to-day reality becomes the location of where God's living and active presence can be seen.

Again, this is not vividness for the sake of merely capturing people's attention or keeping them from drifting off. Instead, and once more to invoke what James K. A. Smith wrote about in *Imagining the Kingdom*: we perceive reality in storied ways. We are narrative animals who arrive at whatever feelings we have at any given moment and who draw conclusions about our lives not through objective analysis of facts and figures and statistics but through the hard knocks (or through the experiences of elation) that just are the sum total of our story on any given Wednesday afternoon or Friday morning. If you *tell* me some people are lonely by virtue of seldom encountering other individuals, I will understand what you mean. If you *show* me an elderly Meals on Wheels recipient eating a microwaved dinner in front of a small TV set, I will feel what is being conveyed on a visceral level and instantly connect it to any times I have ever had sitting by myself in an empty apartment, along with all the attendant emotions I felt back then, too. Of course, for some who listen to sermons, they will not need to recall *past* experiences of such isolation—they will connect to their immediate experience in the moment.

In recent years many of us in ministry have become increasingly aware of certain groups of people to which the church has in the past paid scant attention: singles and those dealing with same-sex attraction or other forms of sexuality that tend to leave them isolated and alone. Most pastors know now that they should not always speak in their prayers and sermons as though everyone listening to them was happily married or enjoying some kind of long-term relationship that most church members would regard as typical or "normal" in some sense. Singles, the divorced, gay people, and others who deal with something in their lives that may mean they live alone need to know they belong in the church's fellowship. My former congregation took the step of renaming one of its dinner fellowship groups from "Dinners for Eight" to "Dinners for Nine" so as to allow the math to work for people who were not part of a married couple to participate without feeling out of place. That was a small thing to do for the sake of pastoral sensitivity—and all things being equal it was a logical thing to do—and yet the need to make that name change had to be specifically pointed out to us before we realized how necessary it was.

Of course, pastoral sensitivity and awareness also means that we should not assume that just because someone is unmarried or not in a conventional family environment for some other reason, that this person is some Eleanor Rigby type who is dying of loneliness. Pitying people or assuming the unmarried *must* be miserable can be as bad as—if not worse than—speaking from the pulpit in ways that seem to make the assumption that everyone hearing the sermon or prayer is married or otherwise attached. But the fact that sometimes we need to have it pointed out to us that fellowship groups in the church should not be premised on people showing up in pairs highlights the need in our sermons to stay alive to the fact that sometimes "the lonely people" of society are sitting right in the sanctuary, hungry to know that their lonely plight is seen by God and that God, by God's Spirit, can minister to them in that situation, too.

Before ending this section, perhaps one other kind of loneliness of which pastors can be aware should be briefly mentioned, as it is increasingly becoming a facet to our lives: the loneliness that comes to people who live with a spouse struggling with dementia. As people live longer and longer thanks to advances in medicine, more and more people are getting diagnosed with Alzheimer's disease and other forms of dementia that can render these people strangers even to spouses with whom they have lived happily for decades of married life. As the subtitle of a May 2012 *New York Times* article aptly put it, "A Rare Form of Dementia Tests a Vow of 'For Better, for Worse.'" The article profiled a man named Michael French who came down with "frontotemporal dementia," a condition with no treatment options, but one that systematically destroys whatever the person with the disease had once been. In the case of Mr. French, until the doctors figured out what was going on, his wife considered divorcing him because he did not seem to be the man she had married. And in many ways he wasn't. She stayed with him but found what many people testify to be the case when dealing with dementia: you can feel totally alone in your own house even though the other person is still physically present.[20]

Of all the forms of loneliness and isolation that preachers can consider and weave narratively into sermons that seek to minister to people in pain, this particular form of experience counts as one of the most pastorally acute. As pastors listen to the stories told to them by congregation members in such situations, and as they connect this to thoughtful films and documentaries and newspaper profiles dealing with the same difficult phenomenon, another whole avenue of pastoral care through preaching will likely open up, and this in turn will provide the opportunity for what has become a refrain in this chapter: the chance for God's saving and comforting grace to become active in the hearts and lives of hurting people.

Conclusion

We began this chapter noting that even young children have a firmer grasp on this life's hardships than we sometimes give them credit for and that this same perception is more than definitely present in the parents, grandparents, uncles, and aunts of those kids, too. But keeping in mind the real-life situations of trouble into which sermons must speak may not be as automatic or inevitable for preachers as some might think. Those of us who grade student sermons in seminary know that with routine regularity those early sermons of many seminarians—even those sermons that have some very fine things going for them—fall short on the pastoral sensitivity scale. The reasons are obvious: some students have not yet had wide experience in life from which to draw pastoral insights, even as many students write seminary sermons with the classroom in mind instead of an actual congregation filled with hurting people with real names and real life stories.

Sometimes it seems that the seminary sermons that fail to address the pains of real life do so in no small part because the students themselves did not grow up hearing sermons that attempted to get at life's hardships. Some of us have heard sermons from preachers who are keenly adroit at aiming their sermons squarely at the knots and complexities of daily life in a fallen world. But many of us have also heard sermons that are "timeless" in the worst sense of the word: they could have been delivered anywhere, anytime in the last two thousand years in that they are devoid of specificity.

Thomas Long once ran across a trove of sermons from a Scottish preacher of a previous generation. Long found the sermons to be very fine in their exegetical insight, and they had a good bit of stylistic flair, too. Long admired the sermons and was prepared to commend them to others as good models of excellent preaching. But all that changed when Long came to realize that although every one of those sermons had been delivered in Great Britain during the darkest days of World War II—days when Britain could at any moment have slid into the abyss of Hitler's nightmare visions for the world—not one single sermon ever acknowledged all the fears that people in that congregation surely brought with them into worship across all that time. There was no address to those grieving the loss of sons in the military or those who had relatives living in London or other cities that were being bombed to oblivion night after night. The sermons were indeed timeless in the worst sense of that word: because they did not fit the time and place in which they were actually delivered, they were finally of little use for any time. To hark back to the *Great Gatsby* line mentioned in the introduction, such sermons may have been all true, but they just possibly didn't matter.

Good preaching does indeed need "more reality." This chapter has addressed that need in terms of dark and difficult matters of human life. Thankfully, however, the reality preachers bring into their sermons does not end there—because there is yet the reality of God's grace in action that also needs to be brought into sermons in a narrative fashion, and to that good news side of our life's reality before the face of God we turn next.

Chapter Three
Showing Grace

For the preacher, there may be no greater privilege than having the weekly opportunity to reveal to the congregation—or perhaps to remind the congregation—of where the active presence of God and of his grace are in their midst. As part of the weekly proclamation of the good news, the Sunday sermon enables listeners to celebrate the ongoing work of God in this world—to celebrate in ways that generate hope and joy.

Grace is the very heart of what makes the gospel's good news so very good, and that grace is ultimately seen in the resurrection of Jesus from the dead. Resurrection means life, not death, has the last word. Resurrection means Jesus is the living Lord and, through the Holy Spirit, Jesus remains active in the world today, rolling back sin and evil and preparing to usher in the fullness of the new creation. Seeing signs of the presence of Jesus's grace is, therefore, to be expected in the life of God's people. If Jesus is the living Lord as we confess him to be, then we know hope can crop up in situations that would otherwise be filled with despair, love will triumph over hate, clarity will come where there would otherwise be only confusion, and gentleness and kindness will melt hearts in a world that is otherwise so filled with brutality and cruelty. These things will happen in a world ruled by the resurrected Christ. These things will happen *because* the resurrected Christ is on the move.

In the previous chapter we saw that preachers need to be adroit at understanding all the situations that bring people a sense of trouble in their lives. But naming such troubles is a key move in preaching in order to provide the opening for God's grace to enter all that with the saving hope of the gospel and the living presence of Christ Jesus. Proclaiming exactly this hope and joy of grace is at the heart of preaching.

But, as most any preacher will confess, if it is true that proclaiming grace is a great privilege, it presents also a great challenge. Sadly enough, trouble is sometimes easier to detect than grace. The daily news provides an up-to-date litany of woe in this world. Grace and the living presence of Jesus, however, are not reported on quite as fiercely or routinely. Seeing the places where God is at work in the world today requires the eyes of faith, and sharpening our vision for just that kind of spiritual perception will be the focus of this chapter. How can we better and more regularly see the presence of God?

Grace in the Bible

Getting better at perceiving the presence of grace is in some ways a key point of the Jacob stories in the book of Genesis. Jacob eventually discovered that if God shows up often enough in a person's life, even the most hardened person might eventually change into someone softer, more gracious, and more readily able to sense the presence of grace just generally. Because at several key junctures in the life story of Jacob, God shows up unannounced and does something that at once startles Jacob and makes him thoughtful.

It began at a moment when, if you were Jacob, God might well be the last being you'd want to bump into. Having just deceived his father Isaac (with the conspiring help of his own mother, no less) and thus having just cheated his older twin brother Esau out of a family blessing that Esau had every right to claim as his own, Jacob goes on the lam. Although his mother Rebekah was a chief instigator of the whole affair, the plot she and Jacob hatched and then executed resulted in a scenario in which Rebekah knew it was highly likely that her one son would murder the other. Since Rebekah had no interest in seeing the old story of Cain and Abel repeated with her two boys, she sends Jacob packing, knowing that she'd perhaps never see him again.

Jacob runs for as long as he can that first day, until finally collapsing in a state of exhaustion so complete that he sleeps like a baby, despite having to use a flinty rock as a poor excuse for a pillow. Jacob then dreams of a ladder or staircase extending from heaven right down to the very spot where his head was resting uncomfortably against a stone. Angels were coming and going on the ladder and at the top was a presence Jacob knew to be almighty God.

Instead of, as a reader might expect, scolding Jacob for the devious deception he had just pulled off, God actually makes promises to stay with Jacob and, more startlingly, God also promises to fulfill the covenant God had started long ago with Abraham, and God would do this through no less than Jacob. Considering what, all things being equal, shifty and deceptive Jacob *could* have heard from a God of truth and justice, these words must have seemed particularly sweet to Jacob. Once he wakes up, his first words are ones of astonishment: "God was here in the place and I didn't even know it!" So Jacob dubs the spot "Bethel" or "God's house" and then—true to his crafty form—goes on to say to God that *if* (and only if) God one day managed to bring Jacob back to his father's household in safety, *then* Jacob would worship the God of Bethel as his God. Until that time, however, apparently all bets were off.

Surprise divine appearance number one in Jacob's life did not quite do the trick in getting Jacob's spiritual house in order. He was still bargaining with no less than God, hedging his bets and taking a "wait and see" attitude toward what God had promised.

Fast forward a couple decades and Jacob is once again on the lam, this time from the wrath of his Uncle Laban, whom Jacob had also scammed and (literally) fleeced in various ways across the many years he lived with and worked for Laban. With nowhere else to go, Jacob decides to return home and face the music with Esau. Although Jacob could hope that the years had softened Esau's fury, Jacob was taking no chances. According to Genesis 32 (and to riff on Frederick Buechner's classic reimagining of this story), Jacob morphed into a kind of General Eisenhower preparing for D-Day as he divided up his men and mapped out a strategy that he hoped would minimize the possibility for open combat with Esau and maximize the potential for a happy ending.

Having done all that he could by using his wits and cunning, Jacob once again lies down to sleep, this time on the banks of a river called Jabbok. Suddenly a stranger jumps Jacob in the dark, they wrestle all the night long, and only as the first light of dawn begins to break on the eastern horizon does Jacob come to realize it's been some form of no less than almighty God with whom he's been kicking and gouging in the mud and the blood all night. This time he names the place not "God's house" but "Peniel," or "God's face." Once again God showed up in Jacob's life in a most surprising time, place, and manner.

This time, however, Jacob would not have to wait long to find God showing up yet again in his life. It would happen that very morning when he encounters his long-estranged brother Esau. As it turns out, Esau no longer bore Jacob any grudges. He'd long forgiven his squirrely little brother and much to Esau's surprise, he had even missed Jacob over the years. So when Esau approaches Jacob the morning after Jacob's all-night wrestling match, when Jacob sees his brother, Jacob knows that this time he's seeing God with his waking eyes. In one sense, it's just Esau, of course: his smile was gap-toothed, his red hair and beard still looked like they'd never come into contact with a comb, and he was still a bit of the bumpkin he'd always been (which was why Jacob had always been able to scam the guy without even breaking a sweat). Yet when this man approached Jacob full of the grace of forgiveness, Jacob knew in a heartbeat where he'd seen that face of grace and love before: it had first been at Bethel and just now Jacob had seen that face of grace up close at Peniel. "To see your face," Jacob gushes to his brother, "is like seeing the face of God" (Gen 33:10).

In other words, to see Esau was to be right back at Peniel.

Apparently, even if a person is as crafty, stubborn, and prone to live ever and only by his own cunning, as Jacob was, if God shows up often enough in that person's life, the time finally comes when that person becomes able to see God even in other people and in other places much more often than would otherwise be the case. The big surprises of God's gracious presence can train a person's eyes to see many smaller surprises of grace in the workaday experiences of life. At least it worked for Jacob. It even got to the point that by the end of Genesis, those with well-trained spiritual eyes could see God's face on *Jacob's* face.

In Genesis 48 Jacob is nearing the end of his life, and so his favorite son, Joseph, brings in Jacob's grandchildren, Manasseh and Ephraim, to receive a blessing from Jacob. Knowing the protocol of their culture, Joseph put the older boy, Manasseh, next to Jacob's right hand, since the older had to receive the greater blessing. But at the last moment Jacob crossed his arms and placed his right hand on the younger boy's head and his left hand on the older child. When Joseph tells his father he was making a mistake in giving the greater blessing to the younger child, Jacob looked up and, peering over top of his crossed arms, he smiled at Joseph—perhaps he even winked—before telling Joseph that he knew exactly what he was doing. God is in the business of upending expectations in life and no one knew that better than Jacob. Had Joseph looked closely at his father's grizzled old face that day, he would have caught sight of the grace of his Uncle Esau also, and beyond that the grace of the God who long ago wrestled Jacob to the ground at Jabbok and appeared at the top of a ladder at Bethel. It was God's face, all right, and thus another surprise appearance of God's own grace.

If we can see God's gracious presence often enough in the big things in life, eventually the Holy Spirit opens our eyes to see God in the ordinary moments and in the faces of everyday folks, too. But this was something that was true not just for Jacob and any number of other characters we may encounter in the Bible: this is something that every preacher should want to be true for all those who listen to his or her sermons every week.

Grace in the Sermon

Sermons should so regularly work to reveal the surprising presence of God and of God's grace in our world that over time people become trained to start to spy God on their own in all kinds of places and circumstances.

But this does not happen automatically—preachers need to be intentional at working on this feature to their sermons. Sometimes, however, it simply does not happen. When Paul Scott Wilson wrote *The Four Pages of the Sermon,* he noted that a key reason to come up with a sermon template that concluded with "Grace in the World" was because in his observation of altogether too many sermons in North America across recent years, Wilson detected a dearth of sermons in which God ever showed up. God was *mentioned* in most all sermons, even as a goodly number of sermons were good at detailing God's past actions when God did lovely things for people with names like Miriam and Isaiah and Mary Magdalene and Bartholomew. But God was seldom depicted as having done anything *lately* for people with names like Phyllis or George or Harold or Judy.

But if preaching is fundamentally about proclaiming the good news of grace through Jesus Christ—if preaching is first and foremost a heralding of the gospel—then sermons need to display the active, ongoing activity of the God who is in the process of making all things new by reconciling all things to himself through the blood of Jesus the Son. Preaching may well accomplish a number of other aims as well, like helping people understand scripture and encouraging people in their lives of discipleship. But at its heart preaching proclaims the hope and the joy that come because of the grace that saves us through Christ's death and resurrection.

Looking for Grace

A good sermon will display an awareness that on any given Sunday the people who come to church do so from a variety of often difficult circumstances: the brokenness that often sours relationships within families, the disappointment and frustration that attends those who see their dreams slipping away, the complexity with which sin often worms its way into people's lives, the loneliness that characterizes the lives of so many people who pass their days longing for a friend. As suggested in the previous chapter, when these daily realities are sketched in sermons, the listeners who know that this describes their situations become hungry for the word of God that can address them in all those forms of pain and dysfunction and disillusionment. And if the preacher does a good job in getting at that grain of real life through the use of well-told stories and specific imagery and concrete details, then it becomes imperative in the sermon to take the next step and be *equally* vivid in showing how and where the grace and the presence of God can show up in those situations.

Therein lies one of the greatest challenges of the preaching craft. The starting point is focusing on God and on what God is doing.

As indicated in the previous chapter, although it is no cinch for preachers to get into people's hearts and lives by providing vivid stories of trouble and hardship, at least trouble and hardship are relatively easy to find most days. Open a newspaper, click on the CNN website, peruse people's Facebook status updates: stories of war and terrorism, cancer and sick children, natural disasters and heinous crimes abound. Pastors often need look no further than their next counseling session with a parishioner to hear about the ways by which life is proving to be a big disappointment to this or that segment of the congregation. A thoughtful survey of the faces assembled before the pastor in worship each Sunday or a thumbing through of the church's pictorial directory can also be enough for most pastors to summon to mind all manner of life's hard knocks.

But finding stories of grace, being able to lift up vignettes of where God and God's Spirit are active in the midst of the congregation and in the wider world, frequently proves to be much more difficult for most pastors. God's grace, after all, doesn't grab headlines and seldom constitutes "breaking news" on any cable news channel. Yet it remains a vital task in preaching to find those stories and to lift them up in celebration week after week. We have all heard sermons—and as a preaching instructor I have read a good many student sermons—in which all of the sermon's color, liveliness, and specificity run in the direction of detailing bad news and trouble. In such sermons grace and hope get passing mention, even though the pastor may try hard to assure people that there is reason to have hope because God is on the move.

But when it comes to naming the specific nature of that hope or pointing to an actual incident where that hope was on vivid display as God is depicted as showing up and actually doing something wonderful, some sermons come up short. Recall the sermon excerpt used in chapter 1, in which a student went on and on to assure people that God fights for us today and wins battles over the false gods of our age even as God won battles over the false gods in ancient Israel. Everything that was mentioned in that sermon was true, but the specifics of when, where, and how God was winning such battles today—and so providing even a hint as to how the average listener might be able to see and so celebrate such a gracious spectacle in the coming week—were wholly absent. Grace was, therefore, left in the abstract, which is a terrible place to leave grace!

Even as Jacob was able to move from seeing God in special places to being able to spy God in more ordinary situations, so those who listen to sermons need to know that God's grace is real, it is tangible, it can be seen and felt and known in specific ways. The stories of grace in action that pastors tell in their sermons can accomplish the very same thing that vivid stories of trouble can do: help people see themselves in the picture. But in the case of presenting grace, enabling people's ability to see themselves in the picture becomes a powerful act of pastoral care as people experience hope and joy in ways they will be able to carry with them long after any given sermon is finished.

Grace in the Everyday

This chapter is about identifying some examples of stories that show God's grace active in the world today. Telling such stories in sermons provides the necessary specificity that people need both to know that God is with them in their lives and to celebrate that same grace when next they see it showing up sometime on a Thursday afternoon or a Tuesday morning. But before detailing the kinds of grace and grace stories that we will consider, perhaps it would be good to note something that preaching students often misunderstand.

When students (and sometimes active pastors, too) hear about what we often refer to as "Page Four" stories of grace from Paul Scott Wilson's sermon template in *The Four Pages of the Sermon*, sometimes the impression is formed that the only stories that qualify for "Page Four" have to be big, bold stories.[1] Some think that finding "Grace in the World" will mean always locating stories that rise to the level of Mother Teresa's amazing work or be the equivalent of someone's walking on water or having an almost physical encounter with the living God. A while back a former student called me from the church where he was serving to tell me that after only about a year-and-a-half of preaching a new sermon or two every single week, he was clean out of Page Four stories. "Now what?" was the essence of his question. After talking to him for a bit longer, it soon became clear to me that he had indeed been restricting his Page Four stories of grace to grand narratives of astonishing power in which God all but showed up in physical form or did the equivalent of writing a message on a wall or instantly curing an untreatable cancer that not two days earlier had shown up on an MRI as being present in nearly every organ of that person's body.

If those are the only stories that could ever qualify as illustrating the active presence of God and of his grace in this world, then even the most well-read and savvy preacher will indeed run out of them sooner or later (and probably sooner). Thus I suggested to this former student what I had hoped had been clear all along: namely, that he look for Page Four stories in much more ordinary, mundane circumstances. Not only are those stories easier to find within the life of almost any congregation, the everyday nature of those stories will actually provide more hope and joy for people than the grand narratives. After all, if grace in any given preacher's sermons gets restricted always and only to Mother Teresa or to walking on water, who in the congregation could have much hope of seeing such grace in their lives during an average week? But if people can begin to understand that the grace of God can show up on their front porch when someone brings a potato chip tuna casserole one evening because someone in the house is sick and so this fellow church member just wanted to lend a hand with dinner, then the chances of seeing evidences of God's grace will increase dramatically.

Years ago when my daughter was just three-and-a-half years old, she developed a mysterious limp, almost a kind of drop-foot kind of gait, which was first noticed by the women who ran the daycare she attended a couple days a week. The limp soon became something worse, as she could barely even drag that one foot along, and very soon after that the pain began in earnest. One trip to the emergency room and a subsequent trip to a clinic revealed no answers, and the pain was getting worse. Finally our own pediatrician was able to see her and within minutes he correctly diagnosed a significant case of osteomyelitis, an infection of the ankle joint that if left untreated would become a life-threatening condition.

So began an entire week in the hospital with needle aspirations of the ankle (and those were every bit as awful as they sound) and IV antibiotics, followed by three weeks at home with round-the-clock antibiotic infusions through a port that had been surgically installed in her subclavian artery before we left the hospital.

Needless to say it was a stressful time for us as parents (although when you spend a week in a pediatric hospital wing, you soon see many parents dealing with far, far graver situations with their own precious children).

For some reason I still preached at the morning service on about the fourth day of my daughter's hospitalization—probably my elders offered to get someone else and probably I stolidly told them I could do it (one does learn eventually to take people up on such offers!). But I led that service feeling exhausted, and I confess there was an extent to which I was just "going through the motions." After the service I was greeted in the church's narthex by a half-dozen three- and four-year-olds from my daughter's Children in Worship class. The kids handed me a large piece of cardboard onto which they had glued a big "Get Well" card for my daughter. Each child had put his or her hand in paint so as to leave a handprint, underneath which was that child's name. The card's words had been written by the teacher: "Julianna, You are in God's hands." I was overcome with emotion and gratitude to these kids and immediately transported that card up to my daughter's hospital room.

A few weeks later in a sermon I was talking about where we find God showing up in our lives, where we can see God active in a world that is otherwise so filled with trouble and brokenness. So I told this story of grace:

> A few weeks ago we were gathered here for our morning worship service as usual. I brought to you a greeting from God at the beginning of the service and left you with a blessing from God at the end. In between we sang to God, prayed to God, and I preached a sermon in which, as usual, I talked a fair amount about God. But I didn't really see God or feel his presence that morning, I confess, until I walked into the narthex after the service and was handed this card made by our three- and four-year-olds in Sunday school. And suddenly there was God, right here in our own church of all places! There was God showing me his face and assuring me of his presence through all these little paint prints of wee hands from the

children of this congregation. Who knew? Like Jacob at Bethel I nearly said, "The Lord was in this place and I did not know it!" But he was. He always is with us wherever we are, and God shows up and works through people and events we could scarcely guess at. What a blessing to serve the living God!

Although I generally resisted telling personal stories in my sermons, this was a vignette of grace that needed to be told precisely because it was not finally my story as an individual, but all of our stories as we can all tell similar anecdotes from our lives. But the point is that it was also an ordinary, everyday story: the kind of thing others had no doubt also experienced and the kind of event that still others could very well encounter at some point.

In what follows, some of the stories I will share about grace in the world today may trend toward unusual and powerful stories of God's grace in action. Such stories do need to be told now and then in preaching, especially since those stories can also connect with smaller examples of such grace in the lives of those listening to the sermon. But preachers should not restrict their grace vignettes to only grand moments in the life of faith—even stories of God's actions in comparatively ordinary events can be told with great power. As St. Theresa of Avila once said, it's more than enough most days to discover "Christ among the pots and pans" of life.

The God Glimpse

At the high school that both of my children attended, one of the religion teachers has an annual assignment for ninth graders: they have to write an essay called a "God Glimpse." To fulfill the assignment the kids have to summon to mind a time and place in their experience where they sensed that God was doing something special. The resulting essays are rarely about anything other than "the pots and pans" of life just mentioned. Kids catch a glimpse of God when they see other kids going out of their way to be kind and helpful to another student who struggles with some physical and mental limitations. Kids catch a glimpse of God when their daily bus ride takes them through a stretch of the city that two years before had looked on the verge of collapse from urban blight, drugs, and crime, but that was recently renovated by a Christian housing organization so that every house along a three-block stretch now looks brand new and is occupied by families with children. "It's like Easter every time I ride down the street," as one put it.

This, in turn, reminded me of a story my colleague John Witvliet told from a conference he once attended, in which the pastor of a church did his own kind of "visual ethnography" (as referred to in chapter 2) by asking students to use their phone cameras to take pictures any time they saw something they believed revealed God at work. Eventually before every worship service at this church, the pastor was able to project one such photo a week as a way to frame the worship service as an encounter with the living God—the God who is doing *this*, for instance. The photos included pictures of soup kitchens, of a teacher with an arm lovingly draped around the shoulders of a crying student, of a child whose face shined with a delighted smile as she sported the new pair of tennis shoes she'd just received from the church's clothing ministry.

In chapter 2 we considered the sociological practice of "photo elicitation" in which sociologists conduct research into people's lives and hobbies and vocations by having people snap pictures from their lives across a certain period of time. Every photo elicits a specific story that together with the rest can help tell the larger story of a person's life. The church version of this "photo elicitation" just considered accomplishes the same thing but in this case specifically reveals stories of grace, of God's ongoing activity in the world through the Holy Spirit of Christ. Any given specific picture may also be generative in eliciting so many *more* stories from all the various people who view such an image of grace and who then begin connecting it to things they also see in their everyday lives.

Grace in Jesus's Parables

As I have contended all throughout this book, because we are fundamentally storied creatures—because we grasp reality and grapple with reality again and again through narrative frameworks—depictions of God's grace in action cannot be limited to declarative statements in a sermon no matter how earnestly, often, or loudly they are spoken by the preacher. People need to connect to God's active grace in the world through stories, through vivid and detailed examples of what it looks like when God shows up to do a gospel work. In the previous chapter we divided up various kinds of trouble, suggesting that most of those forms of pain are already present in Bible stories, even as they regularly showed up in the parables of Jesus. The Bible and Jesus's own parables are, not surprisingly, also the font of any and all forms of grace one could talk about, too.

If we think just about Jesus's parables, we see that grace often showed up in one of several ways: first, grace was discovered in surprising places and coming through surprising people. Think of the treasure hidden in the field: people would just stumble across the kingdom of God and the work of God in very unlikely locations and sometimes even when they were not looking for it. Or grace would come from an unlikely source: an unjust judge who feared neither God nor people but who did the right thing, or grace came from a lowly and despised Samaritan who becomes a font of goodness and who stood in stark contrast to the other characters in the story, from which one would expect more but who did nothing but pass by. The surprise of grace is often that it shows up where you least expected to find it.

Second, grace in Jesus's parables came when ordinary expectations were reversed, and so conventional wisdom was upended. When the wandering son's father bowled him over with forgiveness and acceptance that came so swiftly the boy did not even have a chance to deliver his well-practiced repentance speech, expectations for who deserved what were overturned. When the denizens of the town square earned just as much for their paltry one hour's worth of work as the industrious "early bird gets the worm" folks who labored for twelve hours, all calculations as to merit were reversed. When the greasy tax-collecting scoundrel goes home justified even as the uppity Pharisee leaves the temple under the scowl of heaven, religious conventions and the meaning of salvation were upended in ways that could give hope to even the lowliest of persons listening to that parable. Grace often comes when everything we thought we knew or had reason to suspect would be the typical outcome of a given situation gets reversed and we see the world and other people in a whole new light.

Third, in Jesus's parables grace often showed up as a hidden power that is at work in ways we often overlook but that are steady and sure and, for this very reason, are laden with hope for our world and our lives in it. When we are told that the kingdom is like yeast that disappears completely into a lump of dough but that mysteriously affects the whole thing, we are assured that we don't always have to see grace to know that it's active. When Jesus tells us that the kingdom grows from tiny seeds and keeps on growing even when we sleep, when Jesus tells us that against all odds the shepherd really has left behind the bulk of his flock to seek out the one sheep that got lost, then we know that there is no stopping God's grace in this world, even as people who feel lost at any given moment can know that even if they have not yet been found by the shepherd, he may well still be on his way in a relentless pursuit of those who need his love and care the most. Grace is always active, even if below the surface and in ways we may not be able to detect at any given moment.

Surprising people and places, reversals of expectations, a hidden power and presence that is relentless: these are some of the key ways grace showed up in Jesus's parables, and if all of that was good enough for Jesus, it is surely more than good enough for sermons today. As just noted, many of the stories preachers can tell in their sermons that will access these facets of grace will come from the context of ministry, as pastors and parishioners alike encounter

God's grace and then tell each other about it. But preachers can also seek to stay in touch with narratives of grace when they see examples in literature, books, films, and the news. Even in settings in which a consciousness of God's Spirit is not obvious, we can often spy goodness flowing out from surprising people and places, reversals of how life usually goes, and the quiet working of God's Spirit in many ways.

Images of Grace in Art

Some preachers doubt that fiction or films can reveal grace—grace, some claim, needs to come from true stories, not from novels or screenplays and should perhaps clearly be *Jesus's* grace and not generic graces in life. And it is true: fictional stories lack the character of witness or testimony, even as most of such depictions of grace are somewhat generic in the sense that the stories themselves may not connect the dots to God. Lyric moments in a film or novel just "happen" but no one in the story credits this to the working of God's Spirit (even as it would be fully possible to view the film or read the novel and likewise see no need to invoke anything spiritual). This is a point worth granting to a degree.

Still, I contend that as with vignettes of trouble, so also depictions of grace from books and films can be highlighted inasmuch as they resonate with real life and give people of faith the chance to see similar instances in their own lives—instances when they can and will see the connections to God's living presence in their lives. Yes, true stories, authentic witness, personal testimonies all have great power and pastors need to listen for such stories and encourage people to share them with one another. But preachers need not limit reminders of grace to just this. After all, would it not count as another surprise of grace to discover—as my colleague Roy Anker terms it—"God at the movies"? As just noted, however, the key is not merely to present vignettes from novels or films and just leave them at that, but to connect such examples to also those real-life scenarios that people experience every day.

Thus, as with locating vignettes of the trouble and pain that people need to hear articulated in sermons, so finding narratives of grace is a task preachers need to do intentionally and on a regular basis. Paying attention to what God is up to in the world helps preachers reveal stories that people might otherwise miss in ways that will generate hope as members of the congregation realize again and again that they serve a living God whose Spirit is incessantly on the move. When those who listen to sermons can see themselves caught up in this grand program of gospel and kingdom work, they are assured that never did Jesus speak a word more vital than when he told his disciples, "Surely I am with you, always, even to the end of the age."

The joy of preaching is pointing out the myriad ways by which our Lord keeps that promise.

To See Your Face Is to See the Face of God

Jacob could never have guessed that his reunion with Esau would be an encounter with the face of the same God he had just met at the Jabbok River. Yet there it was: the face of God shining through Esau's ruddy complexion. Thankfully Jacob was by no means the last person to encounter the living God in surprising people and places. But sometimes everyone is helped when their eyes and ears are attuned to be alive to such encounters with God's grace, and the stories preachers tell in their sermons are a key avenue by which the Holy Spirit equips listeners to discover the surprises of kingdom grace in their own lives. Since in his own parables Jesus often had God at work in some of the least likely of characters, it may well be true that there is no limit to the possibilities of where God may show up and in whose life God gets gospel and kingdom work accomplished.

Memoirs of Grace

Preachers can find stories of the incarnation of grace in many places, including in memoirs written by pastors, doctors, and others who have spent their lives witnessing grace show up right in the middle of powerfully difficult circumstances. A lovely pastoral vignette comes from Richard Lischer's memoir of ministry, *Open Secrets*. I once used this anecdote in a sermon from Matthew 7 about prayer and about how Jesus tells us to be very bold so that we ask, seek, and knock without being shy in so doing, because we know—as Jesus says in this section of the Sermon on the Mount—the Father is never annoyed when his children come to ask for bread or for anything else they may need. When we pray, I said in this sermon, we know that God is faithful and will always draw near to those who pray, even in places we might not expect. It was a lesson Lischer and two members of his congregation learned in a powerful way in a very dim and unexpected location. Here is an excerpt from the sermon in which I used Lischer's story:

> In most every way that counts, the bread God gives us again and again at the Lord's table may just count as the ultimate answer to every prayer you or I have ever uttered or will ever utter. "Which of you if your child asks for bread will give him a stone?" Jesus asks. Yet every time we pray—no matter what we are asking for—at the end of the cosmic day, what we are really seeking is exactly this bread of life that just is the body and blood of our Lord Jesus Christ.
>
> Whatever we get or don't get in and through all our long hours of praying, there is ever and again *this* bread. And when by the Holy Spirit the Father hands us this bread, we know that we are already now receiving every last thing we could ever possibly want or need. What we get when this Father hands his children this bread is life, and life abundant at that. Because whenever we pray, the Lord is surely with us, and he has this bread in his hands every time.

In his book *Open Secrets*, Richard Lischer tells of his first three years as a pastor in a small rural town in southern Illinois. Fresh out of school, he had been in his new congregation only a short time when the phone rang at 3 a.m. It was Ed Franco saying his wife, Doral, was at St. Joe's hospital with a ruptured gall bladder. Surgery was imminent and things were shaky. "We need you here, if you can," Mr. Franco said. So Pastor Lischer jumped into the car and took off. He found the Francos in an alcove just off a main corridor of the hospital, flanked by a dingy curtain and a red fire extinguisher on the wall. Ed was nervously patting his wife's sweat-pasted arm. The Francos were a childless, middle-aged couple who never missed church but whom Pastor Lischer had not yet gotten to know.

As he approached the gurney on which Doral was lying, Lischer saw Ed and Doral looking expectantly at him. It was then Lischer realized he'd forgotten his prayer book, his Bible, and anything else that might help him figure out what he was supposed to say in this situation. "Doral" Lischer wrote, "was the most frightened person I'd ever seen, and she was looking right at her pastor!"

It was *very* quiet in the alcove, until Pastor Lischer croaked out the only thing he could think of. "The Lord be with you," he said. "And also with you," Ed and Doral replied in unison, as though they had been waiting for just that. "Lift up your hearts," Lischer intoned. "We lift them up to the Lord," the Francos shot back. And suddenly, Lischer writes, the *Lord* himself was in that alcove. He was the Lord of the alcove and suddenly much that had been disheveled and fevered and sweaty was put back together. Then they prayed to the Father, and soon Doral was wheeled away into the OR, calmer and somehow now ready for surgery. Whatever happened, at least they knew the Father was there. They knew. They'd prayed to him after all.[2]

N. T. Wright once observed that in the Lord's Prayer, we begin with the line, "Our Father in heaven." But, Wright noted, the Father is not just the place where we start, the Father is where we want to end up. The Father in heaven is not just the place to begin, it's the place to end; it's the starting line and the finish line all in one.

Instances of Grace in Bible, Film, and Literature

So very many people in the church can testify to just such a surprising instance of grace, in which God showed up in a dim alcove, at a Starbucks, while walking through the mall. But the same types of surprise discoveries of God occur all through the stories we find in scripture, too. For instance, in a sermon I preached on Joshua 2, the congregation came to see that God can even show up at a brothel and preach a sermon through the madam of the establishment while he's at it. For whatever the reason (though one could dimly guess at a reason) the text of Joshua 2 tells us that the spies Joshua dispatched to scout out the city of Jericho went directly to Rahab's place. While they were there, the city got wise to their presence and so began to search for them. Rahab hides and protects them and even provides them with an escape route out of the city. But before the spies leave, Rahab gives them what amounted to a little homily about how great the God of Israel is and how the people of Jericho knew the story of the Exodus and how this told them that any God as great as Israel's God would not fail to help God's people. It's hard to know what the spies thought they might hear a person like Rahab say, but that she became a spokesperson for the power of their own God simply has to count as one of the greatest surprises of the entire Bible. No wonder God went on to let Rahab play a key role in the establishing of the family line that would one day produce no less than the Messiah himself (see Matt 1:5)!

Oddly enough, it reminds one of the movie *Pretty Woman*, in which Julia Roberts plays the prostitute with a heart of gold who falls in love with a playboy billionaire played by Richard Gere. He, of course, falls in love with her, too, and through her begins to find a meaning and purpose to his life he had never before known. In the closing scene of the movie, he goes to the prostitute's apartment to rescue her from her tawdry life, enacting her lifelong fantasy of being the princess in distress who is rescued by the shining knight on a white horse (or a white limousine in this case). Once the billionaire takes the damsel into his arms in the movie's final moment, the apparently one-way sexist trappings of the scenario get undone after the billionaire asks, "So what happened after he climbed up the tower and rescued her?" "She rescues him right back," is her reply. After Rahab is rescued by Israel when her city is attacked, she could well say the same thing: through her God will rescue Israel and the whole world, too.

God shows up in surprising people. God also shows up in some of those very same people in surprising *ways*. One writer who has consistently revealed what end up being portraits of Grace is the neurologist Oliver Sacks. Many of his stories show what could best be described as a kind of grace at work in people whose lives seem otherwise disabled and disoriented. In a sermon on Psalm 42, in which I was talking about all the hope that emerges from that psalm's line, "Therefore I will remember you," one of Oliver Sacks's stories titled "The Lost Mariner" became an apt illustration of God's work in unlikely places and people:

> In one of his many memorable clinical vignettes, neurologist Oliver Sacks tells us about Jimmie, a man whose memory somehow became a sieve. Jimmie remains forever stuck thinking it's 1945. Harry Truman is president, the war just ended, and this ex-sailor believes he has his whole future to look forward to. Sacks reports that Jimmie is a very nice, affable fellow with whom you can have a good conversation about this or that. But if you leave the room after visiting with him for two hours and then return a short while later, he will greet you as if for the first time. Now, of course, that is simply tragic all by itself, but even more interesting is Dr. Sacks's observation as to the overall effect that this temporal vacuum has on Jimmie: he has no joy. Jimmie is joyless in that he is confined to an ever-changing, yet finally meaningless, present moment. With nothing old ever to look back on and with nothing new ever to look forward to, joy is simply impossible.
>
> Curiously, there is one time when Jimmie displays something akin to joy after all, one moment when the vacant look on his face is replaced with something that Sacks can describe only as a look of completeness and of hushed calmness. This happens whenever

Jimmie takes communion in chapel. Sacks once lamented to one of the Catholic nuns who runs Jimmie's nursing home that Jimmie had lost his very soul due to the disease in his brain. The sister reacted with outrage! "Come back tomorrow," she told the doctor. So the next day Sacks returned around the time they were celebrating Mass. And to Sacks's amazement, Jimmie was able fully to participate in the service, reciting the familiar lines, saying the prayers, and then going to the communion rail to receive the wafer and when he did, Jimmie's face was a picture of calm and, yes, of joy. God was at work in Jimmie in ways that made Jimmie himself a living, breathing, walking, talking showcase display window of a very surprising grace. Sacks knew there was no good neurological explanation for this. But perhaps grace is its own reason.[3]

Perhaps it is a mark of how spiritually jaded we have become that we can be jolted by a gracious working of God even in the midst of God's own holy sacrament! It is possible that one reason we sometimes fail to see the grace of God on active display is because we have allowed repetition or routine to rob us of the ability to spy the ordinary miracles that take place in worship, preaching, prayer, and sacrament every single week. Sometimes it takes a person like Jimmie to clarify for us what in fact happens all the time to all kinds of people, even if often it is on less striking display than in the case of a damaged person like Jimmie.

Grace among the Needy

Sometimes we do see the common more clearly when it comes in more extreme circumstances, as may be true in another striking clinical story told by another physician-author who sometimes spies God's grace and God's presence showing up in surprising places. Richard Selzer once told the following story, which I in turn once used to round out a sermon on Matthew 10, where Jesus tells the disciples, "Anyone who welcomes you welcomes me." The sermon suggested that if the link between the disciple and the master is this snug, then people might well be able to spy Jesus in all kinds of places and people. Whether he himself could put a name to it, Dr. Selzer once saw this gracious truth in action:

> When it comes to delivering the good news of the gospel, we want to be identified with the message. We need to be identified with it and with the Jesus at its core. Jesus said that if people reject us and persecute us, then it should be because of the Christ in us. But if they accept us and what we have to say, then that will be no credit to us but will likewise be because of the Jesus in us. And sometimes, once in a while, when people spy that holy Son of God in something we say or do, the results can be nearly sacramental in the ways by which God's own Son is suddenly present.
>
> The surgeon and writer Richard Selzer once saw something like this. One day, Selzer writes, he had to remove a tumor from the cheek of a young woman. After the surgery, the woman lies in bed, her postoperative mouth twisted in a palsied, clownish way. A tiny twig of the facial nerve had been severed in the operation, releasing a muscle that led to her mouth. Her young husband is in the room along with the surgeon. The woman asks, "Will my mouth always be like this?" "Yes," the doctor has to tell her, "the nerve was cut." She nods and is silent, broken. But the young husband smiles gently and says, "I like it. It's kind of cute." And all at once, Dr. Selzer writes, I *know* who this young husband is. The doctor sensed the presence of "a god" in the room that day, but essentially what the doctor saw was Jesus in the man. He saw Jesus in the man's gentleness and love. And then he saw Jesus afresh as the kind husband bends down to kiss her crooked mouth, carefully twisting his own lips to accommodate her lips, showing her that their kiss still works and always will.[4] "If they receive you, they receive me." That's what the man said. The Jesus in me. The Jesus in you. The one they must see.

It should come as no surprise that sometimes doctors and those who work in situations of extreme hurt and pain and illness can so readily testify to seeing God and God's grace show up in people's lives. Because, as we thought about in the previous chapter, where is the grace of God needed more than precisely in situations of the very hurt and trauma out of which many people come to church every week and the pain of which those same people carry with them into the worship space? In chapter 1 we read the story of the little boy with leukemia who was frightened by the stranger at his door until he finally recognized the stranger as no less than Jesus himself, tenderly present to welcome the little boy into the kingdom.

That true story reminds me of a fictional story from an episode of the classic TV series *M*A*S*H*, set in a mobile army hospital during the Korean War. One day the doctors receive a patient who believes he is Jesus Christ. Arnold Chandler had been a bombardier in an airplane and he had dropped altogether too many bombs on men, women, and children he did not know and who never did anything to harm him. So one day his mind snapped and he decided that this was not who he was, he was not a killer named Arnold Chandler. He was Christ the Lord. The situation was tragic, of course, as this was clearly a mental condition that would require much therapy to overcome so as to restore Chandler to his true identity.

At one point in the episode the psychiatrist called in to talk to the man said, "You say you are Christ, and yet here you are in an army hospital in the middle of a war. What would Jesus be doing here?" With tears streaming down his cheeks this otherwise mentally damaged man replied with words that would actually be as true as true could be were they spoken by Jesus: "I am Christ the Lord. Where else should I be? These are my children." Similarly, where else do the people who listen to sermons every week need to locate Jesus, if not precisely in the midst of war, cancer, familial dysfunction, and nursing homes. Preachers who want to help people find Jesus in those places will listen carefully for testimonies from members of the congregation who have such stories to tell, even as they pay attention to what people on the front lines of suffering—doctors, hospice chaplains, first responders—write and say about encounters with the presence of God and of his grace that they have had or witnessed.

The strategy for preaching that underlies having preachers exposed to such stories is clear: sermons can help listeners be more attentive to the activity of God in their own lives when those listeners see lyric examples of that divine presence in stories like the ones we just considered. Pastors, listen closely to the testimonies of others, as those are often the occasions to see the presence of God's grace on the move today.

Gracious Paradox

In the previous chapter, when detailing examples of trouble in people's lives, the Alexander Payne film *About Schmidt* was brought forward as an example of the pain and disappointment people sometimes feel when looking back on decades' worth of work in a career that ends up looking, in retrospect, as though it did not make any meaningful difference to anyone in the world. The retired actuary Warren Schmidt is a good example of people who spend their later years in retirement looking back on their lives with more regret than gratitude. In the film, however, there is a subplot that throughout most of the movie appears to be one part an injection of humor into an otherwise dim storyline and one part a cinematic device that allows Warren to tell his story through narrative voiceovers.

Early in his retirement and with nothing to do, Warren passes some of his days in front of the television, surveying the daytime TV landscape of game shows, talk shows, and reruns of old series like *Dick Van Dyke* and *Bonanza*. One day, however, he lingers over an infomercial narrated by the actress Angela Lansbury. It is a plea for viewers to "adopt" a third world child by becoming a sponsor who would send in twenty-five dollars a month to support a specific child, whose photo and information would eventually get sent to anyone who responded to this offer. Warren takes an interest and so sends away for the information. A couple of weeks later a large envelope arrives in the mail, and included in the mailing is a picture of a little black boy from some faraway land. The boy is named Ndugu. Along with his monthly support check, Warren is encouraged to write Ndugu letters in Warren's role as the boy's foster father.

Thereafter in the film the content of those letters becomes the device by which viewers hear Warren's voiceover observations about his life, including his feelings when his wife suddenly dies and his fears that his only daughter is marrying a loser who sells waterbeds for a living. The humor emerges from the fact that Warren's letters to the little boy are often wildly inappropriate, sometimes expressing anger and hostility in language hardly suited for a six-year-old, and at other times expressing wishes that are wholly outlandish given Ndugu's impoverished existence (as when, following a visit to his college alma mater, Warren writes to Ndugu his hope that maybe one day Ndugu, too, will be able to pledge a fraternity just as Warren had done at his university).

But then comes the movie's final moments. Warren drives home alone from his daughter's wedding in Colorado where, indeed, she married a man Warren does not like. As he drives the final miles home and then enters his disheveled but empty house, Warren's face is a mask of sorrow and disappointment. As a retired actuary, Warren knows that he will soon die, and he can even run the actuarial equations that pinpoint the likely timing of his final demise.

Sitting at his desk, Warren sorts through his backlog of mail, only to encounter a letter that clearly was mailed from some international location. Opening it, he finds a letter from a Roman Catholic nun who works at the place where Ndugu goes to school and lives. She tells Warren that Ndugu had recently been sick but was now better, thanks in part to Warren's financial support. She also says that although Ndugu cannot read or write, he enjoys having Warren's letters read to him and, what's more, Ndugu made a drawing for his foster father that Ndugu hopes he will enjoy. Warren carefully unfolds a crayon drawing showing an adult—Warren no doubt—holding the hand of a little boy who is smiling. Immediately Warren breaks out into the first full-blown smile of the entire film, even as he begins to weep tears of joy as he realizes in that brief, shimmering moment that maybe he's made a bit of a difference to somebody after all.

This is an image of grace. It is a grace fueled by a complete reversal of what is expected both for the character of Warren Schmidt in the film, but also for us viewers who had concluded that the entire Ndugu subplot was a minor part of the movie. Yet from this unexpected source a grace emerged that upended expectations. Of course, this is just a movie and a fictional storyline that have no apparent interest in making people think about how the living God might bring such moments into a person's life. But such a depiction does have the kind of lyric power to help keep one alive to the surprising possibilities of God's grace showing up in real life and from sources (and people) we would never have guessed at or been able to predict in the abstract.

The sudden turn toward grace, the unexpected assurance that a person is not alone but that God is at work after all, despite what someone might otherwise conclude about her life at the moment: these are the moments when joy happens, when hope makes a powerful comeback. Thus these are moments worthy of celebration in the church and through the sermons people hear in worship. Like Warren Schmidt riffling through an ordinary stack of mail containing mostly bills and junk promotional flyers, it sometimes happens that suddenly you encounter an envelope with a note or a card from a fellow church member or a faraway friend. Maybe the card inside says no more than a pat Hallmark-like phrase such as "Thinking of You," and yet upon reading those words you know with a certainty that defies description that you are hearing the very voice of God through that card. You had been lonely that day. Maybe you'd been feeling isolated for a long while. Most people are not even aware that you've been feeling that way but now suddenly and unbidden here is a card that says, "Thinking of You," and much though you are glad to learn that your friend Shirley or your fellow church member Dave is thinking of you, far greater is your joy in sensing that the real message here is that *God* had not abandoned you, either. God too, is "Thinking of You."

The Surprise of Grace

Grace often comes on us unawares, when we were perhaps least looking for it, much less expecting it. When it does appear in our lives, grace comes not despite the problems we face or the trials that may abound in our lives on any given day, but right in the middle of all that, as a reminder that the one who is in us and for us is greater than the troubles of the day. That seemed to be Jesus's point, too, at the end of Matthew 6 when, after already telling his followers to not worry about food or drink or what may come the next day, Jesus says that we are to seek the kingdom despite the fact that "each day has enough trouble of its own." Jesus concluded one of the most famous passages about worry and hope not with some Pollyanna-like statement that if you just look at it from the right angle, every single day is just splendid. No, each day contains plenty of trouble. But grace comes even so.

Some years ago in a Thanksgiving Day sermon, I talked about the surprise of grace, how hard it can be sometimes to give thanks during a time of war and economic recession when the news most days is rather unstintingly bad. I also talked about how even a saint like Mother Theresa—it was revealed after her death—endured long, long years of "the dark night of the soul," during which she felt God had stopped communicating with her in any way. As the sermon concluded, the lyric conclusion to Katherine Paterson's adolescent novel *The Bridge to Terabithia* served well to talk about grace's reversal of expectations even—or is it especially?—when things sometimes look rather bleak:

> So today I cannot tell any one of you to be thankful without also recognizing and validating the reasons why some of us feel a bit muted on this Thanksgiving Day. In another place Paul says that we Christians talk about hope precisely because we do not yet have the full reality of God's kingdom. If we did have all that lush and lavish joy right now, we wouldn't have to *hope* for it, we'd *see* it.
>
> Hope endures while the longed-for reality is not yet here. Faith is the tether, the bridge, that makes us grab onto God's will

for us even when we can't see it. Mother Teresa used to tell her community of missionaries, "Keep smiling!" but given who she was, her saying that was not trite (the way it might be if Katie Couric or Oprah were to say it at the end of each show). Given her own dark night of the soul, Mother Teresa spoke those words as signs of hope in a still-dim world.

Last summer I read the wonderful youth novel *Bridge to Terabithia* by Katherine Paterson. In the story, an eleven-year-old named Jess spends his days hoping for nothing more than to be the fastest sprinter in fifth grade, even as he tries to avoid the annoyances provided by his pesky and nosy little sister May Belle. One day Jess meets Leslie, a new neighbor just down the road and a new member of his fifth grade class at school. Leslie is a charming tomboy sort of girl with a wonderful imagination. One day she and Jess make a rope swing across a creek and, on the far side of that creek, create a fantasy kingdom called Terabithia. In this kingdom of make-believe, Leslie is queen and Jess is king. They read the Chronicles of Narnia and think spiritual thoughts in honor of the divine spirits that populate the Terabithian firmament. Leslie's imagination helped Jess to imagine a new world, too.

But then one terrible day the rope swing breaks, Leslie falls, and is swept away by the creek's current to her death. Jess's young world is shattered by an event his mind cannot fully absorb. Leslie is gone. Terabithia has lost its queen. But somehow Jess finds it in himself not to let the dream die along with Leslie. So he builds a bridge to Terabithia, laying some old planks across the creek. As he completes the bridge, suddenly that annoying little May Belle is there again, spying on him and being nosy as usual. "Whatcha doing, Jess?" she asks. But this time, rather than shoo her away, Jess says, "It's a secret, May Belle. But I'll tell you it when I finish."

And so after the bridge is complete, Jess places some flowers in May Belle's hair and leads her across the bridge. To someone with no magic in them, the bridge would have looked like no more than a few silly boards across a gully, leading nowhere. But imagination makes the difference, and so as Jess leads his annoying sibling across he says, "Look! Can't you see 'um? All the Terabithians standing on tiptoes to see you." "*Me?*" May Belle exclaims. "Shhh, yes," Jess replies. "There's a rumor going around that the beautiful girl arriving today might be the queen they've been waiting for."[5]

Through an act of simple kindness to an otherwise annoying sister, Jess created an emblem of what grace can look like in life. Thomas G. Long once wrote that if it seems strange to see something as simple as "kindness" listed as a fruit of the Spirit, perhaps that is because we fail to see the underlying power of what kindness is actually all about. C. S. Lewis also once noted that if we could but see our every neighbor for who she or he really is—if we could see what in our Father's kingdom we will each become by the grace of our salvation—then we would see in every person a being of such shining luminescence we would be tempted to fall down in worship. We are kind to each other, Long said, as an eschatological act of deference toward people who are really made just a little lower than the angels and crowned with glory and honor.

Most days people don't feel that way about themselves, and we surely too often forget it about our neighbors. But even as May Belle could not have guessed she'd be hailed as any kind of a queen, so we too often forget that we are children of God, siblings of our older brother Jesus Christ himself, and every once in a while a grace comes our way as someone reminds us that we are not finally just weary people who live in a disappointing world of frustrations and broken dreams. No, we are kings and queens in waiting. Preachers need to point this out regularly and often. As Paul often wrote to the Corinthians, so pastors today should be in the habit of looking at tired and troubled people and saying, "Do you now know who you are? One day you are going to help rule the galaxies along with Jesus as image bearers of God who have been restored to your original glory and honor!"

Seeing Grace as the World Right-Side Up

Grace means that what we see around us—what people regard as the normal, natural way the world works—is very often the upside-down version of reality from God's perspective. In preaching, therefore, pastors look for those stories and images that reveal the world as being different than what the newspapers can show or from how life gets presented on television dramas—the world is different from all that because the world is ultimately saturated with the presence of God if only we have the eyes of faith to see God on the move. Ironically, having a longing to experience stories that upend typical expectations or that reverse the way life usually goes is by no means unique to churchgoing people. As it turns out, telling such stories is very much a stock-in-trade practice in even Hollywood. Talk to any expert on screenwriting or storytelling in the movies and you will soon discover that most of the movies that "work" narrate stories that involve a reversal of expectations, a redemption of a seemingly unredeemable person, a transformation of a character from bad to good.

At a conference sponsored by Fuller Theological Seminary in 2012, I had the opportunity to meet and hear from two experts in the film industry: Pixar's Academy Award–winning writer/director Pete Docter (who among other projects made the films *Monsters Inc.* and the Oscar-winning *Up*) and a screenwriting expert, consultant, and teacher named Bobette Buster. Both know the power of the reversals of grace and both pointed out how frequently just this shows up in the best stories as told by filmmakers.

Hence in *Schindler's List*, a womanizing war profiteer named Oskar Schindler—who seems to fear neither God nor man and who freely parties with Nazi thugs—somehow transforms into the savior of thousands of Jews who honor him and declare him to be among the world's most righteous of persons. In *Field of Dreams*, Ray Kinsella is led to build a mysterious baseball field in the middle of an Iowa cornfield—a field of dreams on which, somehow, long-dead ball players come back to life. Along the way in the story, he meets up with a once-famous writer named Terrence Mann who has sunk into a life of bitterness and cynicism. Before the story is finished, not only does this strange ball diamond redeem Mr. Mann back to his better self, Ray gets reunited with his estranged (and long-dead) father in a way that reverses the way such relationships usually end. Having spent his youth rejecting baseball as a way to needle and hurt his father who adored baseball, in the movie's last scene, Ray says, "Hey, Dad—wanna have a catch?" This scene, and the larger film of which it is a part, is designed to awaken one not to the living presence of God in one's life but to the upending of life. A scene like that reminds us that Jesus told similar stories of reversals when he was trying to show us God's active presence and so one could be reminded of a time when Jesus told a story that upends every expectation: when the prodigal son's father bowls the boy over with hugs and kisses at the end of Luke 15.

God's grace active in the world today means that the way things are—or even the way things have always seemed to be—does not have the last and final word on anyone's life. If movies are any indication, there is a longing deep inside almost everyone to see life turn out differently than might otherwise be expected, to locate (as Bobette Buster said in a lecture) "the extraordinary in the ordinary" in ways that transform those who see the grace that surrounds us. As noted at the outset of this chapter, there is perhaps no greater joy in preaching than getting to tell the stories that show God in action in the world today.

Grace Is Where We Live

At the outset of a sermon on John 11 and the raising of Lazarus, I mentioned a scene from an Annie Dillard short story, in which a family is sadly gathered at an open grave to commit a loved one's body to the ground. At one point the minister invokes the familiar words of 1 Corinthians 15: "Where, O Death, is thy sting?" The reciting of that verse causes one family member to raise his eyes from the ground so as to survey the sorrowful faces of his fellow family members. As he looks at them, he can see also behind them row upon row of headstones there in the cemetery. He thinks to himself, "'Where, O Death, is thy sting?' Why, it's just about everywhere, seeing as you asked." In the sermon, I then used that line, "It's just about everywhere, seeing as you asked," as a refrain that I repeated probably ten times in the course of the message, as the sermon pondered the relentless presence of death in our world and, yes, in also our church communities. The sermon then ended this way:

> In commenting on John 11 Frederick Buechner once pointed out that sometimes people who go through so-called near-death experiences profess to not being completely happy that the doctors pulled them back. Many have said that they saw a bright figure standing in the light and that they wanted to approach that figure but were cut off when the heart defibrillator yanked them back to this world. For them it felt less like "near death" and more like "near life."
>
> Well, as Buechner imagined it, maybe that bright afternoon in Bethany when Lazarus emerged blinking into the Palestine sunshine, only to see Jesus standing there in the light, maybe Lazarus was at first not sure which side of death he was on! Was he walking toward eternity or back toward earth? Some of you have seen the fine film *Field of Dreams*, in which long-dead baseball players somehow come back to life to play on a mysterious baseball field that Kevin Costner's character, Ray, had built right in the middle of an Iowa cornfield. When one player steps out onto the ball diamond, he says to Ray, "Is this heaven?" to which Ray replies, "No, it's Iowa." "Funny, it looked like heaven to me."
>
> So also maybe Lazarus at first asked Jesus, "Is this heaven?" "No, it's Bethany." But maybe it looked like heaven to Lazarus just because Jesus was there. Perhaps as much as anything just that is the point of John 11: whether we live or die, we are the Lord's, because he just *is*, right now, the resurrection and the life. That will have enormous meaning when the roll is called up yonder by and by. But faith understands that tasting Jesus's life and hope doesn't have to wait that long. It is here, now—*Jesus* is here now, and if by faith you can see him, you've begun to taste heaven already.
>
> "I *am* the resurrection and the life." Because of these words from our Lord, when we as Christians get asked by people, "Where

can you find any hope in this world?" we now have the joyful privilege to proclaim the gospel by boldly declaring, "Where is hope? Why, it's just about everywhere, seeing as you asked."

One of the ways by which preachers present the good news of the gospel in their preaching is by looking for those opportunities when we can point to the grace and the hope that surrounds us always, even though it often is lurking just below the surface of everyday life. Pointing to this all-encompassing presence of God should never become a trite or convenient way to dismiss people's real hurts or to diminish the pain people experience, as though if only they could see things differently, they'd instantly feel better and be happy. However, noticing the grace that surrounds us even on the most ordinary of days is part of the bedrock hope we have as believers, and although seeing this grace may not take away the pain of the everyday experiences of many people, it does provide the context in which all disciples carry on in their lives of faith. Because we are narrative creatures, wise preachers will look for those stories that can uncover this all-penetrating grace in ways that will help people see and identify that same grace in the context of their own day-to-day experiences and the narrative of their own lives as individuals, couples, and families.

Grace as God's Glory Theater

Few authors in recent times have done a better job for training people's eyes to see the glory of grace in ordinary life than Marilynne Robinson, particularly in her Pulitzer Prize–winning novel *Gilead*. Through the narrative voice of the old pastor John Ames, Robinson frequently reveals what John Calvin also called the "theater of God's glory" that surrounds us at all times, if only we can see it cropping up inside our everyday experiences. In the story, Rev. Ames got remarried to a younger woman late in his own life and with her he had a son. Ames had long ago given up on the prospect of ever being anyone's father, having lost his first wife at a very young age. But then he does become a father after all, and the wonder of that grace in his life seems to open his eyes to so many other instances of this same phenomenon. The novel is in essence a long series of reflections that Ames hopes his son will read some day long after Ames has himself gone to be with the Lord.

> I'd never believed I'd see a wife of mine doting on a child of mine. It still amazes me every time I think of it. I'm writing this in part to tell you that if you ever wonder what you've done in your life, and everyone does wonder sooner or later, you have been God's grace to me, a miracle, something more than a miracle. You may not remember me very well at all, and it may seem to you to be no great thing to have been the good child of an old man in a shabby little town you will no doubt leave behind. If only I had the words to tell you. There's a shimmer on a child's hair in the sunlight. There are rainbow colors in it, soft beams just the same colors you can see in the dew sometimes. They're in the petals of flowers and they're on a child's skin. Your hair is straight and dark, and your skin is very fair. I suppose you're not prettier than most children. You're just a nice-looking boy, a bit slight, well scrubbed and well mannered. All that is fine, but it's your existence I love you for, mainly. Existence seems to me now the most remarkable thing that could ever be imagined.[6]

Grace in a child's hair. Grace in the colors of dew. Grace in the sheer fact of existence. Or even grace at the breakfast table:

> I woke up this morning to the smell of pancakes, which I love. . . . It is my birthday, so there were marigolds on the table and my stack of pancakes had candles in it. There were nice little sausages besides. And you recited the Beatitudes with hardly a hitch, two times over, absolutely shining with the magnitude of the accomplishment, as well you might. . . . I hate to think what I would give for a thousand mornings like this. For two or three. You were wearing your red shirt and your mother was wearing her blue dress.[7]

Robinson, via her fictional character of John Ames, models for readers a way of seeing the world that notices its shimmering details and that then connects them to the abiding presence of God and of God's grace. Far from some version of viewing the world through the proverbial "rose-colored glasses," this is a spiritual way of seeing that reveals our daily stories to be a part of God's big story.

Grace Transforming Everything

Earlier in this book we noted that the Bible presents narrative or story not as a device but as a statement on the fundamental nature of reality. From God's perspective life just *is* a story, and each of our individual stories fit somehow within that larger narrative that began in the beginning when God said, "Let there be light!" If everything I have suggested in this volume about our nature as storied and narrative creatures is true, then it is neither an artifice nor an imaginative overreaching to see that life—hard and painful though it frequently is—really is drenched somehow by the presence of God and of God's redeeming grace.

Once in a while intimations of this crop up overtly even at the movies, and along these lines I know of no more stunning an image of this sense for how God's presence changes everything than the concluding scene from the Robert Benton film *Places in the Heart*. The storyline of the film, set in Depression-era Texas, is harsh. In an opening scene, the town's sheriff is called away from his family's dinner table to deal with a young African American boy named Wylie who has for some reason gotten himself drunk and is now randomly firing a pistol into the air near the railroad yard.

Wylie is not a bad kid, and the sheriff knows this and so he freely approaches him to ask him to hand over the gun. Wylie clearly intends to comply but then accidentally fires the gun through the sheriff's chest, killing him outright. The boy is promptly lynched by members of the Klan, even as the sheriff's widow, Edna, is left with a too-big mortgage and two young children. As the film proceeds, the widow is harassed by the local banker, who shows no mercy in helping with her finances. She is assisted by a wonderful black man named Moze, who has a keen skill for growing cotton and with his good help, Edna avoids foreclosure for the year by growing a bumper crop of cotton. But Moze's help only upsets the local members of the KKK, who rough him up and chase him out of town.

The film's conclusion is bittersweet—Edna is solvent for the time being but has lost her friend and helper Moze as a result. She's still a widow with small children, and the odds are still against her in a world where the meek don't usually come out ahead. But the very last scene of the film is the one that reveals a surrounding grace that often goes unnoticed in a world exactly as full of troubles as the one this film sketches. The final scene takes place in church. The service begins normally, but then the Lord's Supper is celebrated, as we see the platter of bread cubes and the tray of wine cups being passed person to person up and down the rows of pews. Suddenly people are there partaking of the sacrament, people who, all things being equal, should not be there. The town prostitute is sitting next to the merciless banker. A woman killed earlier in the film in a tornado is also there along with a couple who have now reconciled after an adultery that nearly wrecked their home. Even Moze is back and seated next to a member of the KKK, who passes the bread and the wine to Moze, before he in turn passes the elements to Edna, who then passes it to her dead husband, who then passes it to the boy Wylie, who is mysteriously seated next to the sheriff.

As the picture fades to black, the killer and the victim exchange the bread and the cup and say to each other, "The peace of God." Then the viewer realizes the truth: what we are witnessing is the kingdom of God that is hidden in this world like yeast in dough but that even now is leavening the whole unwieldy lump of our reality. We are witnessing the grace of God that surrounds us always and that even now is reconciling victims, victimizers, old enemies, and sinners of all kinds. God is raising up Abel but also Cain, Jacob but also Esau, Sarah but also Rahab, David but also Saul, Mary the mother of Jesus but also Mary Magdalene, the woman "with a past." The enmity we so often see around us in our families, at work, at school, and even (or is it especially) within our church communities does not have the last word—not so long as the Lord is near and his blessed sacrament is celebrated and his Holy Spirit is on the move. Just below the perception of most of us much of the time there a grace that becomes like the air around us: ever present, necessary for life, but often invisible, at least to the untrained eye.

Whenever I watch this final scene, I weep. I weep not because the movie is itself so lyric—though it is—but because in my mind's eye I connect this to my own story and to all the people in my past whom I have offended or who have offended me, people who at some point told me they'd never speak to me again and stayed true to their word. And so I envision sitting next to them in the sharing of the peace of God through the body and blood of Christ Jesus the Lord, and when I can see my story nestled inside the all-penetrating presence of God's grand story, the hope is renewed that reconciliation and the grace of God are even now becoming—and one day will fully become—the dearest and deepest reality for us all. Sensing already now how this grace permeates our lives and our world—and having that pointed out in the narrative context in which and through which we parse our everyday experiences in this world—wings this truth into my life and into the lives of others in a way no set of propositions or concepts in a sermon could ever accomplish.

Conclusion

In his book *The End of Words*, Richard Lischer makes the case for the power of story, and even the power of the most familiar stories we know, by quoting a few lines from G. K. Chesterton, who wrote,

> It might be true that the sun rises regularly because he never gets tired of rising. His routine might be due, not to a lifelessness, but to a rush of life. The thing I mean can be seen . . . in children, when they find some game or joke that they especially enjoy. A child kicks his legs rhythmically through excess, not absence, of life. Because children have abounding vitality, because they are in

spirit fierce and free, therefore, they want things repeated and un-
changed. They always say "Do it again"; and the grown-up person
does it again until he is nearly dead. For grown-up people are not
strong enough to exult in monotony. It is possible God is strong
enough to exult in monotony. It is possible God says every morning "Do it again" to the sun; and every evening "Do it again" to
the moon; it may be that God makes every daisy separately but has
never got tired of making them. It may be that He has the eternal
appetite of infancy.[8]

Lischer goes on to say that "preaching is one of God's 'do it
again' activities," and then compares this to the adopted child who
repeatedly wants to hear the story of her adoption told exactly as
she's heard it who knows how many times before, just so she can get
to the final part, where she can then ask her parents, "And then out
of all the babies in the orphanage, you chose me, right?"[9] No one
would ever grow tired of such a story, even as Israel and now the
church cannot possibly ever grow weary of the story that centers on
the grace of God by which out of all the peoples of the earth, God
chose us.

In this chapter I have argued that similarly, we can never grow
tired of hearing all the subnarratives of grace that show this same
God still on the move, still at work, still busy in our lives and in our
world today. "Such stories do not entertain, they do something far
better. They *sustain*. They do not inform, they *form* those who hear
and share them for a life of faithfulness."[10] Throughout this book we
have seen again and again that fundamental to the human experience is story. At any given moment in our lives we sum up where
we've been, assess where we're at, and project forward into our future
in narrative ways. At its best, preaching the word of God becomes
a part of—not an exception to—this daily way by which we parse
reality. Those who listen to sermons will come to realize that their
own struggles and troubles are being articulated in the sermon when
they hear stories in whose picture they spy some of the jagged edges
of their lives as well. But then they subsequently are able to see that

the hope and joy of the gospel intersects with this world as they see God on the move in ways that catch up the whole of their lives, too.

Some years ago, when I delivered a series of lectures on preaching in Japan, I drove my translator to distraction by using some of the terminology of Eugene Lowry, from his book *The Homiletical Plot*. Among Lowry's descriptions for what listeners should experience in a sermon are hard-to-translate words like *Oops* and *Ugh*. Those two terms describe what happens to people when they hear the part of the sermon that in this book I have called "trouble" from Paul Wilson's framework. But I have always delighted in the words Lowry used to describe what happens when grace breaks through onto people's hearts as they listen to the sermon, because for those moments of saving joy Lowry says that the congregation's reaction could best be described by a sense of "Whee!" followed by a firm declaration of "Yeah!" as listeners affirm the presence of the Spirit and of the gospel's power.[11]

Personally, I have rarely if ever experienced such emotions of transcendent affirmation when reading a technical manual, receiving instruction on how to repair a dishwasher, or listening to an information-heavy lecture on the history of the Roman Empire. But read to me a story that quickens my pulse, show me a movie clip that depicts a soaring moment of redemption, or simply tell me what a traditional hymn calls "the old, old story of Jesus and his love," and I will very likely respond by standing up and declaring my "Yes!" when I see my story as part of God's grand story. And that is something that is true not just today. To refer back to the hymn just mentioned, it will surely be true in our Father's kingdom: "And when in scenes of glory, I sing the new, new song; t'will be the old, old story that I have loved so long."

Notes

Introduction

1. C. S. Lewis, *The Lion, the Witch, and the Wardrobe* (New York: Collier Books, 1970), 64.

2. William H. Willimon, *Conversations with Barth on Preaching* (Nashville: Abindgon Press, 2006), 161.

3. James K. A. Smith, *Imagining the Kingdom: How Worship Works* (Grand Rapids: Baker Academic, 2013), 108.

4. Stanley Hauerwas and Gregory L. Jones, eds., *Why Narrative? Readings in Narrative Theology* (Grand Rapids: Eerdmans, 1989), 66.

5. Ibid., 78.

6. Ibid., 263.

7. Smith, *Imagining the Kingdom*, 32.

8. Ibid., 59.

9. Thomas G. Long, *Preaching and the Literary Forms of the Bible* (Philadelphia: Fortress Press, 1989), 69.

10. Paul Scott Wilson, *The Four Pages of the Sermon: A Guide to Biblical Preaching* (Nashville: Abingdon Press, 1999).

1. Show, Don't Tell

1. Ron Rozelle, "Balancing Description & Summary," in *Crafting Novels and Short Stories: The Complete Guide to Writing Great Fiction*, ed. editors of *Writer's Digest* (Blue Ash, OH: Writer's Digest Books, 2011), 238.

2. Harper Lee, *To Kill a Mockingbird* (New York: J. B. Lippincott, 1960), 214.

3. John Gardner, *On Becoming a Novelist* (New York: W. W. Norton, 1999), 33–34.

4. Francine Prose, "On Details," in *The Eleventh Draft: Craft and the Writing Life from the Iowa Writers' Workshop*, ed. Frank Conroy (New York: HarperCollins, 1999), 136.

5. Ibid., 141.

6. Nancy Kress, "Keep Your Story Lean," in *Crafting Novels and Short Stories*, ed. editors of *Writer's Digest*, 251.

7. Rozelle, "Balancing Description & Summary," 240.

8. Ibid., 241.

9. Frederick Dale Bruner, *The Christbook: A Historical/Theological Commentary: Matthew 1–12* (Waco: Word Books, 1987), 270–71.

10. Marilynne Robinson, *Gilead* (New York: Farrar, Straus, Giroux, 2004), 9.

11. Richard Ward's updated telling is on the DVD included with the book, *Performance in Preaching: Bringing the Sermon to Life*, ed. Jana Childers and Clayton J. Schmit (Grand Rapids: Baker Academic, 2008).

12. Frederick Buechner, *The Clown in the Belfry: Writings on Faith and Fiction* (San Francisco: HarperCollins), 18.

13. Ibid., 19.

2. Showing Trouble

1. Gary Schmidt, *Okay for Now* (New York: Clarion Books, 2011), 145–46

2. Eugene Peterson, *Leap Over a Wall: Earthy Spirituality for Everyday Christians* (San Francisco: HarperCollins, 1997), 38.

3. Frederick Buechner, *Telling the Truth: The Gospel as Tragedy, Comedy, and Fairy Tale* (San Francisco: HarperCollins, 1977).

4. Paul Scott Wilson, *The Four Pages of the Sermon: A Guide to Biblical Preaching* (Nashville: Abingdon Press, 1999).

5. James K. A. Smith, *Imagining the Kingdom: How Worship Works* (Grand Rapids: Baker Academic, 2013), 14n26.

6. This material was presented by Roman Williams in an on-campus presentation, Calvin College, Grand Rapids, MI, March 2012.

7. Philip Roth, *American Pastoral* (New York: Vintage Books, 1997), 3.

8. Ibid., 423.

9. Joyce Carol Oates, *We Were the Mulvaneys* (New York: Plume, 1997), 3.

10. Ibid., 30.

11. Anne Tyler, *Ladder of Years* (New York: Alfred A. Knopf, 1995).

12. Russell Banks, *Affliction* (New York: Harper Perennial, 1989), 52–53.

13. Russell Banks, *Continental Drift* (New York: Harper Perennial, 1994), 4, 12.

14. Robert Caro, *Means of Ascent: The Years of Lyndon Johnson* (New York: Alfred A. Knopf, 1990), 301–50.

15. Robert Caro, *The Passage of Power: The Years of Lyndon Johnson* (New York: Alfred A. Knopf, 2012), 605.

16. Marilynne Robinson, *When I Was a Child, I Read Books* (London: Picador, 2012), 126.

17. William Manchester, *Winston Spencer Churchill: The Last Lion: Visions of Glory 1874–1932* (New York: Dell Publishing, 1983), 125.

18. William Manchester, *American Caesar: Douglas MacArthur 1880–1964* (Boston: Little Brown and Company, 1978).

19. Taylor Branch, *Parting the Waters: America in the King Years 1954–63* (New York: Simon and Shuster, 1988), 109–10.

20. Denise Grady, "When Illness Makes a Spouse a Stranger," *The New York Times*, May 5, 2012.

3. Showing Grace

1. Paul Scott Wilson, *The Four Pages of the Sermon: A Guide to Biblical Preaching* (Nashville: Abingdon Press, 1999). In Wilson's "Four Pages" model for sermon structure—in which each "Page" is a distinct unit of the sermon—"Page One" details "Trouble in the Biblical Text," and then "Page Two" corresponds to this by highlighting where that same trouble crops up in the world today. "Page Three" looks for "Grace in the Text" to see what God said or did in this biblical text in response to the situation/trouble at hand, even as "Page Four" then looks for an example of when and where and how God is doing or saying the same thing in the world and in the church today.

2. Richard Lischer, *Open Secrets: A Memoir of Faith and Discovery* (New York: Random House, 2001), 61–63.

3. Oliver Sacks, *The Man Who Mistook His Wife for a Hat and Other Clinical Tales* (New York: Harper and Row, 1987), 23–42.

4. Richard Selzer, *Mortal Lessons: Notes on the Art of Surgery* (New York: Harvest Books/Harcourt, 1996), 34–35.

5. Katherine Paterson, *Bridge to Terabithia* (New York: HarperCollins, 1977), 162–63.

6. Marilynne Robinson, *Gilead* (New York: Farrar, Straus, Giroux, 2004), 52–53.

7. Ibid., 185.

8. Richard Lischer, *The End of Words: The Language of Reconciliation in a Culture of Violence* (Grand Rapids: Eerdmans, 2005), 105–6.

9. Ibid., 106.

10. Ibid., 107.

11. Eugene Lowry, *The Homiletical Plot: The Sermon as Narrative Art Form* (Atlanta: John Knox Press, 1975).

CPSIA information can be obtained at www.ICGtesting.com
Printed in the USA
LVOW04s0710240914

405489LV00003B/4/P